THE MOBILITY OF WORKERS UNDER
ADVANCED CAPITALISM

D1606101

The Mobility of Workers Under Advanced Capitalism

DOMINICAN MIGRATION TO THE UNITED STATES

Ramona Hernández

 COLUMBIA UNIVERSITY PRESS NEW YORK

Columbia University Press
Publishers Since 1893
New York   Chichester, West Sussex

Copyright © 2002 Columbia University Press
All rights reserved

Library of Congress Cataloging-in-Publication Data
Hernández, Ramona.
The mobility of workers under advanced capitalism :
Dominican migration to the United States ;
Ramona Hernández.
p. cm.
ISBN 0–231–11622–5 (cloth)
ISBN 0–231–11623–3 (paper)
1. Alien labor, Dominican—United States.
2. United States—Emigration and immigration.
3. Capitalism—United States.

HD 8081.D65 H47   2002
331.12'791—dc21   2001047537

Columbia University Press books are printed
on permanent and durable acid-free paper.
Printed in the United States of America

c 10 9 8 7 6 5 4 3 2 1
p 10 9 8 7 6 5 4 3 2 1

This book is dedicated to my mother, Mercedes Hernández, a woman who barely completed elementary school but whose wisdom was beyond books and formal schooling. To her I owe my respect for women. It is also dedicated to my father, Ramón Hernández, a humble man who learned how to write and read at the age when others go to college and from whom I learned to love others as much as I love myself.

Contents

Tables

Acknowledgments

Several people accompanied me on my long journey in completing this book. My colleague and friend Silvio Torres-Saillant helped me reassess the strength of my arguments with his questioning, his "buts," and his "what ifs." Frank Moya Pons, Paul Attewell, and Mauricio Font read the early version, when the book was still a dissertation. I have been privileged to work with them; their comments and suggestions greatly improved the contents of the book. Thanks to my colleagues at the University of Massachusetts—Boston. Glenn Jacobs, James Green, Quentin Chavous, and Raul Ybarra took the time to read portions of the manuscript. Their suggestions, which emanated from different academic fields, ranging from American labor history to Spanish literature, proved to be decisive in improving the quality and the readability of my arguments. Similarly important were the conversations with Chris Tilly. His insights on the working poor and on the dynamics of the American economy, and his suggestions of specific readings in his field helped me think through the arguments advanced here. And, of course, I am eternally indebted to Frank Bonilla. His life-long work on Puerto Ricans and other Latin Americans provides the theoretical foundation of this book. I have been very fortunate to have had him as a mentor. This book and much of my other academic work arose from his teaching, writings, and many spirited conversations with him throughout the years. Needless to say, the views expressed in this book are mine, and I have the sole responsibility for whatever fault the reader finds in it.

Many thanks to my extended family, Anthony Stevens, Daisy Cocco-de Filippis, Ginetta Candelario, Nancy López, and Belkis Necos, who have given me the necessary support to continue to be focused. Sarah Aponte, the Dominican Studies Institute's (DSI) librarian, and Joel Cruz, a college assistant at the DSI, went beyond the call of duty to locate materials for the book. Ircania Valera, my research assistant, provided technical assistance in preparing the index and keeping me up to date on data relevant to my work. I thank Ana Garcia, my friend and sister, for her trust and the value she has placed on our friendship; her commitment to the well-being of the Dominican people has inspired me to keep going even when my body and my soul have threatened to fail me. *Mi querida* Doña Juana humanized the cold census data that attempted to reflect the struggle of poor working Dominicans.

My deepest gratitude goes to my immediate family. My little brother, Aldrin, my brother in-law, Ramón, my nieces and nephews. They are the greatest family anyone can ever have. Many thanks to my sister, Ana, an amazon who has helped me raise my Alejandro along with her four children. Without her concrete support, her love for me, I know I would not have been able to do as much as I have in the world. The final gratitude goes to my son and my husband. Alejandro, my son, who feels a tremendous sense of pride for the work I do, although it may keep me physically away from him. I have said this before and I will repeat it for as long as I live: my husband has done my job with our son. He has attended the parents' meetings at school and has taken care of our son's meals. I thank him for his love, his unconditional support, and for being the backbone of our family. Without his sacrifice for our family, this book would have taken an eternity to come into fruition.

Finally, Godwin Chu, my manuscript editor at Columbia University Press, should take all the credit for the clarity and the beauty of the writing.

THE MOBILITY OF WORKERS UNDER ADVANCED CAPITALISM

INTRODUCTION

The Mobility of Labor in Response to Demand

What explains the international mobility of workers from developing to advanced societies? Why do workers move from one geographical region to another? Such simple questions, which may elicit a prompt answer from ordinary people or even from migrant workers themselves, have, for a long time, puzzled and preoccupied scholars. A primary explanation for such mobility is provided by the connection between supply and demand in the job market. According to this view, the supply of workers in a given region and the demand for them in another locale explains the movement of workers. Job seekers from less-developed regions feel compelled to migrate to advanced societies where they expect to find use for their labor. Within this frame of reference, the action of leaving home is explained by one of two macrotheoretical paradigms. The first, known as the "equilibrium" theory, views the migration process as the result of the individual worker's own rational choice. The second, known as the "historical-structural" theory, emphasizes macrosocioeconomic changes that are beyond the control of the workers but whose impact creates the conditions which force them to leave.

Receiving societies, in turn, are conceived as areas of labor scarcity. After World War II, the advancement of technology and the changes in production in immigrant countries created the need for a specific labor force to serve in undesirable and poorly paid jobs commonly rejected by native workers. Immigrants from poor sending societies with a high incidence of surplus labor become the ideal pool for such jobs (Portes 1978). Such, then, is the context within which post-1965 Third World immigration to the United States has been generally viewed.

I

Scholarly consensus supports the notion that the shifting of the U.S. economy, from manufacturing to service after the 1950s, generated a bifurcated labor market that mainly required highly skilled and low- or unskilled workers. Earning structures reflected a similar polarization: high-skill jobs were generally well paying, while low-skill jobs paid poorly. A strict rigidity overtook the labor market, lessening the chances of upward mobility among workers. Well-paying jobs increasingly depended on the accumulation of human capital that exhibited sophisticated and specialized knowledge. Low-paying jobs, in turn, tended to draw from a poorly educated labor force whose members disproportionately came from ethnic minority and immigrant groups.

Old industrial cities like New York reflected the economic changes and the polarity—decaying standardized manufacturing production at one end and booming high-tech service production at the other. But the duality also reflected the mushrooming of a new industrial setting associated with low levels of capital and intensive labor, as well as a fast-changing garment industry. Characteristic of this new industrial setting were sweatshops, informal manufacturing, and the production of seasonal goods under subcontracting arrangements. The service-oriented economy also produced a variety of low-paying and low-skill jobs, such as delivery boys, messengers, maids, parking attendants, and retail salespersons. Additionally, jobs emerged through the purchasing power of a new clientele, namely the highly paid workers of the service economy who consumed a variety of custom-made goods, from gourmet food and expensive furniture and clothing to personal-care services (Sassen 1988:145).

A common feature shared by the two booming job markets was their need for a very cheap and politically powerless labor force. The competitiveness of the new manufacturing sector sprang from the effective reduction of production costs. By the same token, the pay structure of the service sector remained polarized, with well-paying jobs at the top, an explosion of low-paying jobs at the bottom, and relatively fewer jobs at the middle level (Harrison and Bluestone 1988). Sociologist Saskia Sassen has argued that a relative shortage of labor among women, blacks, and Latinos has existed since the 1960s, when the labor-reserve army of native workers was considerably undermined by political processes and by economic aid to the destitute provided by the welfare state. The mid-1960s found cities like New York with employers who yearned for a suitable supply of workers, while the immigration of jobseekers grew enormously (Sassen 1984; 1988). The unproblematic rapport between supply and demand in the labor market would seem to imply that once in the receiving society, migrant workers had no trouble finding jobs. One gets the idea that undesirable jobs, rejected by natives, went unfulfilled until new immigrants took them.[1]

II

The international mobility of workers as a direct response to a demand for labor in the receiving society bears some examination. Whether workers move responding to their own initiative or to macroeconomic forces beyond their control, the essential idea is that they enter into a migratory movement in response to a call from the receiving society. That call entails the promise of a job for those who did not have one and a better job for those who had jobs before migrating. Thus workers and jobs appear aprioristically arranged in a union that has the potential for pleasing everyone. This view, however, overlooks the complications and shortcomings of a changing capitalist economy whose main concern is increasing profits.

Standard thought on migration assumes that jobs awaited migrants in the receiving society. From that perspective, the migratory process invariably appears as a successful enterprise on the part of jobseekers whose mobility from society A (the home country) to society B (the host country) gives them the opportunity to become active members of the labor force. By implication, this view overlooks the possibility of marginalization and long-standing poverty among immigrants in connection with their exclusion from the process of production. The arrangement also distorts the nature of capitalist accumulation. The use of technology in production as a way to decrease the need for labor is a regular modality applicable to the system across all capitalist formations. There is nothing that exonerates workers in the Dominican Republic from expulsion from the production process as a direct result of the system's accumulation needs. Nor can we believe that they will easily reenter the process of production in the United States, a country that, like the Dominican Republic, is informed by the same system of production and the same needs of accumulation.

A study of the relationship between Dominicans and the New York City labor market offers a revealing picture. The Dominican case, contrary to what many had imagined, shows a group facing economic hardship as the result of unemployment and underemployment. Once in New York City, Dominicans confront the reality of a changing labor market that increasingly requires workers with skills and training they do not have. As Dominicans came, the jobs they had the best chance of qualifying for were rapidly disappearing, and the competition for them grew. In Washington Heights, the neighborhood with the largest concentration of Dominicans in New York City, peddling various tropical products and other low-price consumer goods has become pervasive. The two largest job markets—street vendors and taxi drivers (whether regulated or unregulated)—appear to have become saturated. As the largest group of workers in Washington Heights, Dominicans often complain about other newcomers, their compatriots included, who come into the area to try to make a living. This scenario seems to defy the presumption of a smooth relationship between supply and demand in the job markets of the receiving society. The precarious conditions of most Dominicans suggest either that the host country did not need workers when Dominicans arrived, or that it did not specifically need the labor of Dominicans.

An Alternative Reading of Labor Mobility

The first argument advanced in this book is that post-1965 Third World immigration to the United States reflects the movement of a surplus labor force to a host country that did not necessarily show a demand for their labor.[2] The fact that immigrants came did not mean that they were all needed or wanted. The proposed argument rests on the following assumptions:

1. The continued internationalization of production via the mobility of capital and other inputs for production generated the use of cheap labor in peripheral nations, thereby reducing the need for labor mobilization across geographies.
2. Structural changes in the system of production, particularly the shift from a manufacturing to a service-oriented economy, led to a restructured labor market that required better educated workers. Low-skilled and unskilled workers increasingly became redundant, since the altered economy had failed to generate enough of the kinds of jobs for which those workers were equipped.
3. An internal labor-reserve army already existed in the United States, consisting of low-skilled and unskilled workers who had lost their jobs through economic

transformation. These workers either failed to reenter the process of production or entered under irregular conditions, economic growth notwithstanding.

4. The accumulation of capital tended to depend increasingly on the use of technology and information, displacing all kinds of workers in the process.

5. The growing influx of immigrants possessing similar demographic characteristics and level of skills, education, and English-language abilities tended to increase the size of the supply of low- and unskilled workers. This tendency made for competition among workers, and it enabled employers to easily substitute them on the basis of subjective criteria, such as sex and ethnicity.

The Changing Economy: No Need For Extra Hands

By the 1960s, it was clear to many that the labor supply had begun to exceed demand. The economic changes, particularly the flight of manufacturing capital out of New York City, had begun to produce noticeable effects. The restructuring process directly displaced jobs in production, as well as a whole variety of other jobs that were tangentially connected to the manufacturing sector. Entire industrial headquarters moved out, and with them went employment opportunities. From 1960 to 1980, the total number of jobs in New York City decreased from 3,538,000 to 3,302,000, a 6.7 percent reduction. From 1966 to 1976, the employment-to-population ratio declined from 55 percent to 48 percent (Torres 1995:193). The manufacturing sector alone, by far the single largest employer up to 1970, lost over 600,000 jobs between 1960 and 1990. This loss, the repercussions of which would be felt among most members of the labor force, would have far more devastating effects among blue-collar, low-skilled, and unskilled workers, for whom the sector provided the greatest number of jobs. From 1970 to 1986, the restructuring led to the elimination of 510,000 jobs in fields that required less than twelve years of education (Kasarda

1985). Furthermore, a vast number of the displaced workers would find no reentry into the expanding service sector.

Scholars believe that the decline in manufacturing jobs caused increased levels of poverty and economic hardship among socioeconomic groups associated most closely with the industry. Sociologist Clara Rodríguez has argued that the high incidence of poverty among Puerto Ricans in the 1960s stems from their displacement from the manufacturing sector, which in the 1960s supported over 60 percent of the community's labor force (Rodríguez 1979:208). Sociologist William Julius Wilson has likewise contended that the emergence of an under-class among blacks is connected to widespread unemployment in the inner city brought on by the disappearance of blue-collar jobs that required less than a high-school education. He adds that new service-sector jobs were not an option for most blacks, who simply lacked the necessary level of education (Wilson 1987).

The scenario described thus far would suggest that the period of economic transformation was a tough time for blue-collar, low-skilled, and unskilled workers. Not only were well-paying manufacturing jobs exiting the city, but the restructuring process seems to have reduced employment options at all levels. Economist Andrés Torres estimated that from 1960 to 1970, the secondary sector lost 10 percent of its share of jobs, declining from 38.8 percent to 29.9 percent. More importantly, the proportion of jobs generated through the development of what Sassen has called "down-graded jobs," associated with the manufacturing and service sectors during the restructuring process and served primarily by immigrants, could not do much to increase the proportion of secondary sector jobs, which in 1980 retained the same number of jobs it had had in 1960 (Torres 1995:48).

In the 1960s, whites began to leave the city. Their flight would accelerate and come to include Puerto Ricans, blacks, and other minority groups in the two decades that followed. By 1970, all those who could afford to exit the city, packed up and left. The census figures indicate that from 1970 to 1980, New

York City lost 10.4 percent of its overall population, a net figure of 824,261 persons. In the meantime, Dominicans and other immigrants, particularly from Latin America, began to come and settle in the city. The newcomers came endowed with similar skills and levels of education. They were young, energetic, and eager to find work. Yet the newcomers found themselves trapped in a city that increasingly lacked the kinds of jobs they could hold. They arrived only to witness the decline of blue-collar jobs and to experience unemployment and disconnection from the labor market. Thus, for many, the act of migrating to an advanced society was not necessarily a passport to the economic progress and social mobility that they thought awaited them.

Emigration as an Expulsion of Workers

The second argument put forward in this book is that emigration from the Dominican Republic corresponded to a government initiative taken during Joaquín Balaguer's first presidency. Though not officially promulgated, the Dominican government deliberately implemented a de facto policy of encouraging people to leave home. Initially, the strategy sought to expatriate political dissidents and revolutionaries, mostly members of the left-wing movement, and others, who, having participated in the 1965 revolution, worried the newly established Balaguer government, the Dominican ruling class, and the United States. Emigration also had a long-term goal for the Dominican government and the power structure, and it had to do with economic development in the country. Emigration provided a pipeline through which the country could systematically eliminate unwanted and unneeded surplus laborers whom the new system of production was unable to absorb. The exodus could thus prevent the eruption of civil disobedience and social unrest caused by an impoverished people who could find no way to make a decent living. In this case, contrary to what has been proposed, the Dominican exodus to the United

States is not a "spontaneous" movement (Massey et al. 1994: 721) but a well-orchestrated event.

Massive emigration from the Dominican Republic to the United States began in 1966 with the coming to power of Joaquin Balaguer. The large contingents of Dominicans who left their native land from 1963 to 1965 came in the wake of political instability triggered by the assassination of dictator Rafael Leónidas Trujillo in 1961, the discontent that culminated in a military coup d'etat in 1963, and a civil war that erupted in early 1965. Upon assuming the direction of the Dominican State in 1966, the Balaguer government tackled two principal concerns: economic development and political stability. Economically, the government implemented a model that eased the entrance of United States investment and tended to emphasize industrial production, commercial trade, and finance to the detriment of agricultural production. Politically, Balaguer put in place a reign of terror that virtually dismembered the opposition through frequent incarcerations, assassinations, and the expatriation of political dissidents. The modernization of the army and the national police forces, with assistance from the Pentagon and the CIA, provided the necessary infrastructure to ruthlessly impose order by the sword in the country, as may be gathered from the fact that Balaguer's first two terms in governments left a toll of more than 3,000 people killed (Moya Pons 1995).

During Balaguer's first twelve-year regime, the Dominican Republic would be characterized by dichotomous tendencies. On the one hand, there was unprecedented economic growth, via the expansion of industrial production and the business sectors. On the other hand, there were growing unemployment levels provoked by the intensification of industrial capital, an inadequate policy of job growth, and the internal mobilizations of uprooted people in search of jobs from the countryside to the city. In the end, Balaguer's economic policies resulted in a growing surplus of laborers not absorbed by the expansionist economy. Similarly, the government gave way to the formation of an urban middle class associated with the expansion of public jobs and the commercial and financial sectors. Its purchasing power activated and expanded the levels of consumption of the internal market, while, concomitantly, growing numbers of the working class, unemployed, and underemployed remained disenfranchised, since they could not afford even basic necessities. From 1970 to 1974, the Dominican Republic experienced the highest rate of economic growth of any Latin American country, with an average return profit in net gains of over 54 percent in the industrial sector.

However, during the same period, the country had an official unemployment rate of over 20 percent. More than half of all able-bodied workers were underemployed. The bottom fifth of the population with the lowest income experienced an extraordinary loss, reflecting a fall of more than half its income. And 75 percent of the people did not consume the number of calories and nutrients required to maintain an adequate diet. Neither the administrations of the Partido Revolucionario Dominicano, which ruled the country from 1978 to 1986, nor that of the returning Balaguer in the period 1986–1990, generated any improvement in the lives of most people at home. During the 1980s, or "the lost decade," in the words of Dominican economist Bernardo Vega, most workers who needed to work for a living suffered. Many were displaced from the process of production by an economy that systematically introduced technology into production and increasingly depended on a labor force that possessed formal schooling and training.

New development policies (i.e., export-led economy and tourism) further internationalized the Dominican economy. The level of importation of foreign inputs increased considerably, producing trade deficits and loss of revenue. The problem of unemployment and underemployment increased in severity. To make matters worse, the large national debt and the country's inability even to pay the interest owed provoked the intervention of the International Monetary Fund, whose severe economic restrictions, particularly in the public sector, harmed the material well-being of many more people. In the process, members of the middle class, who may have remained unaffected before, now suffered displacement. They were affected by the decline of well-paying jobs and by the loss of their purchasing power before an ascending inflation.

Both the United States and the Dominican governments collaborated in fomenting Dominican migration by setting in place the appropriate infrastructure and logistics, from the modernization and expansion of consular services to the expediting of official documents required to emigrate. But both participating actors had different agendas. Through its involvement, the United States sought to rid the small Caribbean country of unruly and deviant political discontents perceived as obstructing the access of U.S. capitalists to the country. Some in Washington may have also believed that the country was in danger of becoming a communist or socialist state. The intentions of the United States government became clear in the role American diplomats played during the tumultuous years after the assassination of dictator Rafael L. Trujillo in 1961 and during the transitional government headed by President Rafael Bonnelly.

The Dominican Republic also sought the emigration of political dissidents. It was a way to disarticulate and eliminate left-wing movements, which at the moment, threatened to disrupt a government that had forced its way in. But for the Dominican power structure it was more than that. Emigration would also function as a permanent channel through which unwanted and unneeded workers would be discarded. The channel would facilitate the expatriation of the relative or absolute surplus population generated by the system of production. Ironically, the shipping out of unneeded humans, subsequently became, through the frequent remittances of the emigrants to their relatives in the native land, an indispensable pillar that has helped sustain the status quo in the Dominican Republic.

The emigration of people as a long-term plan, combined with an extremely persuasive birth control campaign, begun precisely in 1966, targeted the poor, and succeeded in reducing population pressure in the country. Both strategies, one fiercely promulgated (birth control) and the other silently enforced (emigration), sought to regulate the lives of people, particularly those who had (or promised to) become redundant in one way or another. The birth control policy, widely promulgated throughout the country and systematically enforced from 1966 to the present day, propagated a new ideology among poor people. The right to procreation was connected to one's ability to secure a decent living for one's future children. Of course, birth control advisors would have been at a loss for words had a Dominican peasant or unskilled urban worker asked them how in the world they could expect to earn a decent living in a society that was rapidly closing the doors of its job market to them.

Emigration would provide the answer to the question. Stimulating those who could find no job or generate a decent living at home to simply pack up and leave with their children seemed to be the unspoken answer. After all, what was being done in the Dominican Republic was not totally new. The emergent Dominican State of 1966 adopted development policies that had already been put into practice in the neighboring island of Puerto Rico during the 1950s. Government planners had thought that Puerto Rico suffered from an excess of people that exerted pressure on the economy and contributed to the country's high rates of poverty and unemployment. Encouraging Puerto Ricans to leave home for the United States and adopting a birth control policy were the two antidotes prescribed as the cure to the country's economic ills. The development policies generated successful results. An increasing number of Puerto Ricans left every year for the North American mainland, just as the birth rate went down. In the end, almost one third of the Puerto Rican women within reproductive ages had been sterilized.

Just as in Puerto Rico, abandoning the homeland became the order of the day for a vast number of Dominicans. The family planning policy would control the propagation of many of those Dominicans who remained home. During the 1970s, an annual average of 16,000 Dominicans arrived legally in the United States. By the 1980s, the annual average had risen to more than 30,000. In the meantime, many poor people, who had internalized the belief that poverty had to do with their procreation patterns, began to use birth control methods. As a result, we witness the drastic reduction of the fertility rate from 8 children per woman in 1955 to 3.2 between 1990 and 1995.

Life in the Metropolis

The final argument developed in this book challenges the traditional correlation between migration and economic progress. The question of social mobility among migrants who moved from a poor to a richer country has been generally approached from the understanding that people emigrate because they are better off after migration. This assumption is not entirely unjustified. Indeed, one could ask, how the Dominican exodus, other than those individual cases involving political persecution, makes any sense unless the immigrants find some rewards in their quest? Some Dominican migration scholars attest to the social mobility and economic progress among U.S. Dominicans. Their findings clearly suggest that for Dominicans migration to the United States has indeed been a wise move, yielding both material and psychological benefits. Scholars, including Hendricks (1974), Portes and Guarnizo (1991), George (1990), and Grasmuck and Pessar (1991), point to economic progress among Dominicans as being reflected in their ability to find jobs, to become business owners, to acquire basic electronic goods, or to sustain a middle-class lifestyle back in their home country.

The present work has chosen to tackle the following issues: whether the findings of the scholars reflect the nature of the group or isolated instances; the representativeness of the success attributed to a Dominican entrepreneur sector; the demonstrable socioeconomic profile of Dominican women in places like New York City; the presumed elasticity of job markets available to Dominicans; and the validity of assessing the socioeconomic conditions of Dominicans in the receiving society in comparison to their former standard of living back home. The fact that some Dominicans, either through return migration or remittance, were able to sustain a middle-class lifestyle back in the Dominican Republic says very little, if anything, about the current socioeconomic conditions of Dominicans in the United States. At most, the evaluation of Dominicans in the immigrant land based upon their country of origin, outside of their immediate social contexts, can provide only a false sense of their socioeconomic conditions as immigrants. One could safely argue that for many Dominicans migration to the United States has afforded them little more than a shift of scenery. Poor at home, they continue to be poor in the receiving country. Many had no jobs at home, and after leaving, many remain jobless.

In its broadest sense, the assumption of a profitable and successful migratory movement is indirectly supported by the lack of sufficient information on the living conditions of Dominicans in the receiving society. One can also argue that the assumption is sustained by the works of writers who celebrate, for instance, the benefits of self-employment among Dominicans without measuring its rate of failure and other negative side effects. There are those who describe the ease with which Dominicans find jobs tailored to their specific needs and desires, or who measure the extent to which Dominican women have used their ingenuity and strength to raise the living standards of their households in the receiving society.

Moreover, the well-documented reality that the majority of Dominican migrants find dead-end, low-paying, and undesirable blue-collar jobs, if not outright unemployment, is somehow lost in the minds of readers who are informed by constant reference to the precarious living conditions in the homeland without the benefit of comparable information about the often dismal conditions that Dominicans encounter in the receiving society.

There exists a serious lack of data concerning Dominicans as a settled people who are involved in daily tasks and multiple responsibilities in the society where they now live. In the meantime, while lack of information helps to validate the widely accepted assumption that views migration to the United States as a wise move on the part of the Dominican people, questions concerning the living status of Dominicans in the host country remain unanswered. We still need to know whether Dominicans as a group, after thirty years of a massive and continuous migratory movement to the United States that has given birth to settled, old communities, have been able to surpass the socioeconomic levels generally attributed to new arrivals in the receiving society.

We have also found a high degree of selectivity in the information that is brought to the fore. Who they are and what they want as a settled community, for instance, generally stay outside the scope of most Dominican migration scholarship. The reader normally encounters, instead, a systematic discussion of a group of people who remain deeply submerged in the news of their native land. At most, some scholars have granted Dominicans a partial membership and sense of attachment to their new home by conferring upon them the condition of being transnational, or a people who live in two countries.

The scarcity and selectivity of writings about Dominicans in the United States have given way to a lineal and uncomplicated perception about this group. The new land is idealized, and, unequivocally, Dominicans are perceived as a people who have benefitted from migrating to the United States—people who have managed to enhance their socioeconomic position in the homeland as well as in the receiving society.

But, the fact remains that U.S. Dominicans go beyond a precarious past, a transnational identity, or a successful economic position as returnees. Dominican migration has generated realities that are intrinsic to the new milieu. Many of these perspectives are being captured by emerging diasporic voices, such as that of the young Dominican writers Junot Díaz and Juleyka Lantigua. Díaz's stories describe Dominican neighborhoods where the buildings "break-apart . . . [with] little strips of grass . . . [and] piles of garbage around the cans and the dump— especially the dump" (Díaz 1996). Díaz creates Dominican characters whose diet contains "government cheese," narrators who speak of Dominican mothers who, despite their Amazon qualities having "traveled to the East and learned many secret

things, despite their resemblance to "shadow warrior[s]," settled for cleaning houses, minding their homes, and raising children without husbands, and, ingeniously stretching budgets to
clothe their children. Lantigua, on her part, presents journalis-
tic and fictional narratives of immigrants who find themselves
in societies where they learn that jobs are not easily available
and that even the most menial ones, require specific qualifications. Altagracia, one of Lantigua's characters, finds a cleaning
job in a hotel because she "had worked as a maid before. No,
not in a hotel but for affluent Dominicans who liked their
friends on this side of dark and their help on the other" (Lantigua 2000). These are characters who are brave but who also go
insane in the new land. These Dominican characters are not
idealized; they are not immigrant super heroes and heroines.
These are people who encounter the obstacles, vicissitudes, and
challenges faced by those who are poor and marginalized in a
society that has historically blamed the victims and has refused
to view poverty as a social ill rather than as an individual choice.

In this book I attempt to continue filling the gap concerning Dominicans in the receiving society. The idea is to bring the
discussion to a level in which Dominicans are imagined as a settled people. As a group whose complexity reflects those who
constantly go back and forth, as well as those who never get to
leave and are finally being buried here. As such, the emphasis
in this book is no longer what Dominicans do back home nor
what migration means for their relatives in the native land. That
some of them return and that many more wish they could
return home can hardly suffice to show the ways in which
Dominicans continue to live, give birth, die, bury their dead,
and struggle to survive in the new land. The emphasis then is
placed on those who are here—who they are, how and where
they live, and where they need to go in the new society. Here is
a group who consciously or unconsciously is engaged in the
daily task of building permanent homes far away from the land
of their original ancestors.

This book also hopes to provide an understanding of the
Dominican people in relation to other groups in the receiving

society. Here is a view of a people who have limitations and possibilities and who ought to compete for social space within an arena that has no tradition of sharing. The locus is New York City, where more than half of the Dominican people in the United States reside. The book presents an assessment of how they live in the most populous Dominican neighborhood, Washington Heights–Inwood. It talks about the kinds of jobs Dominicans have, and whether workers' earnings are enough to provide for the well-being of their families. There is also an assessment of poverty among Dominicans, of the composition of their households, the arrangement of their families, and their social standing in comparison to other Latinos, non-Hispanic blacks, non-Hispanic whites, and the average New Yorker. Finally, this book is a commentary on those who leave home in search of a better future and the society where they settle.

PART I

Leaving the Land of the Few

I.

THE GREAT EXODUS: ITS ROOTS

Massive emigration from the Dominican Republic began in 1962 after the death of dictator Rafael Leónidas Trujillo, who ruled the country tyrannically from 1930 to 1961. During the dictatorship, international migration was severely restricted, and only a few Dominicans, particularly diplomats and well-to-do people who were known to favor the government, were granted visas. It has been argued that Trujillo's emigration policies were motivated by the desire to prevent discontented Dominicans from attacking and discrediting his government internationally (Canelo 1982:41). Historian Roberto Cassá situates Trujillo's emigration policies within a general context of population increase, which the dictator firmly emphasized during the entire length of his regime. Population increase under Trujillo resulted from the direct intervention of the State in three ways: the systematic encouragement of childbirth, the sponsoring of European immigration, and the strict control of emigration from the country. Trujillo thought that an increase in population would fortify and solidify his regime. In 1920, the population reached 900,000 people, yet by the end of Trujillo's regime it had increased to more than 3 million people (Cassá 1982:572).

Regarding Trujillo's firm population growth policy, historian Frank Moya Pons has noted that Trujillo's regime strongly believed the country to be severely underpopulated, resulting in a shortage of laborers. The assumption that the lack of workers prevented the economic development of the country led Trujillo to encourage the growth of the population. Early in his regime, Trujillo's government encouraged childbearing, along with European immigration, by offering incentives to large families, as a way to remedy labor scarcity (Moya Pons 1977:516).

Regarding population movement during Trujillo, Eugenia George reasons that toward the end of his government, the dictator may have had economic as well as political motives for restricting emigration. By this time, George explains, Trujillo had already confronted strong internal opposition within the country and was also aware of the democratic reforms that threatened to dissolve similar governments in Latin America. Information concerning his regime then needed to be controlled. Concurring with Moya Pons's views of labor shortage during Trujillo's regime, George concludes that Trujillo's control of population movement developed in response to the direct exigencies of a new productive system. She points out that Trujillo's "policies restricting mobility within and off the island were formulated to ensure the supply of skilled workers to the burgeoning import-substitution industries of Santo Domingo, as well as agricultural producers on whom the cultivation of traditional export and food crops hinged" (George 1990:29).

As indicated in figure 1, in 1963, after Trujillo's assassination, the number of Dominicans admitted under permanent status to the United States rose, from 4,603 in 1962, to 10,683. Emigration continued to increase progressively, as witnessed in the annual number of Dominicans who left their homeland between 1962 and 1991. Between 1962 and 1972, the annual mean of Dominican migrants was 11,445. This number increased to more than 16,000 during the 1970s and to more than 30,000 during the 1980s. Similarly, since 1983 the number of permanent residencies granted to Dominicans has exceeded the 20,000 per-country limit set by the United States. In 1991 and 1992 the number of Dominicans admitted to the United States grew to more than 40,000 each year.[1]

The following section examines the forces that motivated Dominicans to abandon their country after Trujillo's death, and, more importantly, why they selected the United States as their point of destination.

Explaining Dominican Migration

In examining the causes behind massive Dominican migration to the United States, researchers have focused on the demographic background of the migrants, particularly their social class status and their geographical region. The pioneering research of Nancie L. González, (1970; 1976), Glenn Hendricks (1974), Chiqui Vicioso (1976), Saskia Sassen (1979),[2] and J. Frank Canelo (1982) characterize post-1965 Dominican migrants as predominantly rural, poorly educated, poor, and mostly unskilled and jobless. Implicit in most of these studies was the understanding that these migrants perceived their movement to the United States as the solution to their socioeconomic problems.

Antonio Ugalde, Frank. D. Bean, and Gilbert Cárdenas (1979) challenged this notion by arguing, instead, that most Dominican migrants were mostly from the urban middle-class sectors of the Dominican Republic. They were not the poorest, nor did they come from the ranks of the unemployed (1979:243–4). Contrary to previous research, which depended on small ethnographic surveys undertaken in specific rural communities in the Dominican Republic, Ugalde, Bean, and Cárdenas's study was based on a national survey of 125,000 people in 25,000 households. The survey was conducted in 1974 by Secretaría de Estado de Salud Pública y Asistencia Social and financially supported by the United States Agency for International Development. Most recent research in the United States has concurred with the findings of Ugalde, Bean, and Cárdenas (Pérez, 1981; Pessar

1982; Kritz and Gurak 1983; Bray 1984; Grasmuck 1985; Báez Evertsz and D'Oleo Ramírez 1986; George 1990; Grasmuck and Pessar 1991; Portes and Guarnizo 1991).

Most of the early authors perceived Dominican international migration as a response to direct internal processes or push factors. Hendricks, for instance, identified economic hardship generated by transformations in the countryside involving mechanization and competition generated by the development of export agribusinesses. Equally important in the uprooting of peasants, however, were the pull factors associated with a chain migration responsible for generating the emigration of entire families from Sabana Iglesia, the rural village where Hendricks conducted his research, and the abundance of jobs that awaited the migrants once in the receiving society (1974:40–70).

J. Frank Canelo cited six reasons behind Dominican exodus. For him, of paramount importance was (1) "the failure of the agrarian reform, which did not provide peasants with the necessary facilities for production, and therefore, for their subsistence" (1982:49). [Author's translation]. Similarly, Canelo added that people left (2) because of political motives, particularly those who had participated in the 1965 revolution and who were fearful of government persecution. They also left because of (3) limited educational resources; (4) the application of old administrative methods in the national economy, which affected the development of institutions and the specialization of the working class; (5) wrong investment policies, which were incapable of creating enough jobs to resolve the serious unemployment problem; and (6) low salaries (:49–50).

González, focusing on factors specifically affecting peasants, offered a clear, detailed explanation of why Dominicans became international migrants. To her, it seemed clear that peasants were pushed out of rural areas into an international migratory process. Dominican migrants were surplus labor produced in the countryside. They had a better possibility of finding a job and enhancing their social standing in a large metropolitan city, such as New York, rather than in a small community (1970:155).

González believed that the progressive division of land into *mini-fundios* (small farms) among inheritors and its intensive use without modern inputs negatively affected agricultural production in the countryside. Also, González noted that other areas were subjected to intensive and indiscriminative deforestation and had lost their agricultural potential (157).

Commenting on the socioeconomic background of Dominicans, sociologist Saskia Sassen noted that "the influx of Dominicans . . . rose in the early 1960s because of political push factors, including Trujillo's murder and later Juan Bosch's revolution in the Dominican Republic." These Dominicans were classified by Sassen as members of the middle class (1987:280). Rural and working-class Dominicans came to the United States in the late 1960s, when the increasing "flow began to include many more persons of lower class origin," leading Sassen to conclude that "a large share of the migrants are peasant and agricultural laborers who formerly would have entered the internal rural-to-urban migration flow but now simply jump that stage"(1987:180–81).

Scholars publishing after 1979 often combine internal and external factors to explain why Dominicans became international migrants. Chiefly, they have advanced two explanations. The first has to do with political factors in both the sending and the receiving societies. Many argued that after the 1965 U.S. military invasion and the subsequent establishment of a U.S.-sponsored government in the Dominican Republic, both nations encouraged migration from the Dominican Republic as a safety valve to expel political dissenters and prevent social revolts (Báez Evertsz and D'Oleo Ramírez 1986:19; Bray 1987:158; Pessar and Grasmuck 1991:31; Portes and Guarnizo 1991:32; Mitchell 1992:90, 108–9). The second explanation alludes to economic factors, including the failure of the development policies implemented in the Dominican Republic after 1966, political upheaval related to economic crisis, salary differences, and the austere measures promoted by the International Monetary Fund (Grasmuck and Pessar 1991:34–46; Báez Evertsz and D'Oleo Ramírez 1986:18, 20; Bray 1987:156–59).

It should be noted that besides the causes discussed above, some authors also link the continued movement of people to the development of Dominican settlements in the receiving society. In this sense, a chain migration based on family or friendship ties becomes a pull factor in the uprooting of people. Thus, Dominicans already residing in the receiving society constitute a direct vehicle for emigration for those who want to leave (González 1970; Hendricks 1974; Sassen 1979; Garrison and Weiss 1987; Portes and Guarnizo 1991). Garrison and Weiss's study shows, for instance, how a paternal aunt who had become a U.S. citizen during the 1940s initiated a migratory process that led to the uprooting of a good number of the Dominguez family, including the aunt's brother and his wife, some of their adult children, their grandchildren, as well as other nonblood relatives who became part of the family through arranged marriages (1987:246–47).

Alejandro Portes and Luis Guarnizo believe that a chain movement does not only continue a process of migration, but it could also become an independent leading cause behind a migratory process. In explaining the causes behind Dominican migration, the two authors contend that irrespective of the forces that may have originally activated the movement, the exodus has continued because once a migratory movement begins, it tends to move in *cadena*, becoming thenceforward a self-feeding process (1991:32).[3]

The Middle Class and the Urban Background: Deconstruction of a False Identity

Thus far, the findings revealed by Ugalde, Bean, and Cárdenas in 1979 regarding the class origins of Dominicans in the United States have dominated the debate. No other alternative postulate concerning Dominican migrant socioeconomic background has been articulated. A concrete implication derived from the wide acceptance of the 1979 model is that U.S. Dominican migrants have come to be portrayed as a monolithic group endowed with high human capital qualities, who move in search of improving their incomes and who do not represent surplus labor in the sending society. A second implication is that international migration from the Dominican Republic is a self-selective process, monopolized by one group who is adversely affected in the native land and has decided to take charge and change their destiny. By implication, the proposed argument takes away the agency from other sectors of the Dominican population; it undermines their need and their desire to change their future.

It is interesting to note that the urban middle-class monolithic perception has remained, even when researchers have encountered signs that would seem to contradict the widely accepted 1979 model. As I will show later, the tendency has been either to ignore the contradictory signs or to present vague explanations that are inconsistent with the reality of their findings. But how accurate are the post-1979 researchers in describing the socioeconomic background of U.S. Dominican migrants?

In a comparative study conducted among urban Dominicans residing in New York City and Santiago in the Dominican Republic, Grasmuck, a supporter of the 1979 model, found that "the New York data reveal that Dominican labor exports draw from a predominantly young, male, educated population" (1985:158). The New York sample was better educated than "the population of the capital of the Dominican Republic [Santo Domingo], known for higher than average educational levels compared to the country as a whole" (159). Their median level of education was eight years. Grasmuck also found that "the overwhelming majority, or 69.8 percent, of the migrants reported that they had . . . been working prior to departure" (159), leading the author to conclude that her "results contradict the impression that Dominican emigrants, especially illegal ones, are predominantly unskilled, unemployed workers" (162). But Grasmuck also found that over 30 percent of her New York sample reported being unemployed prior to migration to the United States (159). Grasmuck's study acknowledges that the rate of unemployment reported in her New York sample exceeded the rate reported in the city of Santo Domingo and Santiago, 19.3 percent and 18.5 percent respectively, during the same period. Such high rates of unemployment prior to migration leads Grasmuck to observe that Dominican migrants in the United States represented an "apparent surplus" in the Dominican Republic, since "they constitute the type of 'human capital necessary to any meaningful type of expanded industrialization" (169).

Yet, a reader who is less committed to the model in question will find in Grasmuck's study the fact that such a high percentage of Dominicans had been unemployed prior to migration had to represent more than just an "apparent labor surplus," or a group of workers who could be incorporated into the process of production at some point during industrial expansion. To the contrary, statistics concerning unemployment in the Dominican Republic indicate that unemployment was consistently high during the 1970s and '80s, reflecting a structural problem rather than a temporary situation of the job market and general economic slow downs. In effect, unemployment has remained high regardless of economic expansion, or economic boom, as reflected during the 1970–1976 period, years of high economic growth and economic expansion in the Dominican Republic (see table 2.1).

From a methodological perspective, a challenge to Grasmuck's findings regarding New York Dominican educational stock is the comparison of two sets of data that cover two distinct sets of circumstances. While the New York survey, consisting of a snowball sample, drew information about working Dominicans "who were employed at the time of the survey in New York City" (151), the Santo Domingo information was extracted from a probability sample, surveyed by Oficina Nacional de Planificación, with a diverse sample group, including ten-year-old minors. In this case, the age variable in the Santo Domingo case and the specificity of the New York sample debilitate a comparison of the two studies.

In a study published in 1986, Roger Waldinger compared

Dominican and Chinese owners in the garment industry and found that Chinese owners were more successful than Dominicans because Chinese firms were larger, older, and more productive (1986:168). He argued that the Chinese were more successful than Dominicans in the business because prior to migration the Chinese had had more exposure to a competitive economy in their country, had a higher level of education, and were generally more urban than Dominicans (178-80). In effect, Waldinger explains that among Dominicans, "most of the owners interviewed were originally from the rural areas in the northern part of the Dominican Republic. On average, they received 9.9 years of schooling; 12 of the 32 owners had obtained a high school education or more. Not all the owners had worked prior to moving to the United States, but of those with work experience, most had been involved in activities of a blue-collar or trading nature. Once arrived in New York, most owners had made a livelihood as garment workers, and the movement from worker to owner was often protracted, lasting on average 14 years" (176).

Waldinger finds that both immigrant groups value education differently. He finds that Chinese owners valued education highly and see it as a tool for their children to move up socially. The Chinese believed that education help their children find a job in a large company and have a better life in the future. The author reports that in contrast to the Chinese, Dominicans did not mention education, or a professional career, as a vehicle that could help their children improve their future living conditions. For them, the prospects of a better life for their children was based on ownership or on developing one's own business (173, 178).

Waldinger does not challenge the 1979 middle-class model despite the clear implications of his findings. As with Grasmuck's study, Waldinger's research suggests that Dominican migrants are predominantly unskilled and blue-collar workers who have less than a high-school education and who could have been unemployed prior to migration. Waldinger's data also suggest that Dominican New Yorkers could be from either rural or urban areas of the sending society. These findings, however, do not seem to figure in the prevalent interpretation of the sociodemographic origins of Dominican migrants. They did not have any affect among the scholars whose works have systematically continued to portray Dominican migrants as members of the urban middle class. These findings clearly show, however, that most Dominicans in the United States do not represent an urban middle-class group as the 1979 model suggests.

A careful examination of the occupational distribution of Dominican migrants in the study reveals that the researchers' own findings on occupation do not support their thesis about the middle-class status of Dominican migrants. Their own "occupations" table reveals that an overwhelming majority of Dominicans did not hold middle-class jobs. In effect, while only 10 percent of Dominican migrants held professional, managerial, and technical jobs, 23 percent held blue-collar jobs in areas such as industrial operations and construction, 19 percent held service jobs, including private household service, 10 percent worked in sales and clerical positions, and 7 percent worked in transportation (242). If occupation was used to indicate the social strata of Dominican migrants, then it is obvious that their occupational distribution does not reflect the migration of a middle-class group, but rather the migration of a more diverse group, dominated predominantly by blue-collar, low-skilled, working-class people.

There are also inconsistencies between the Diagnos study and INS data concerning the occupational backgrounds of most Dominican migrants coming to the United States. While the Diagnos survey found that Dominican international migration was predominantly a middle-class phenomenon, the INS annual reports indicate that throughout the 1970s and '80s the vast majority of Dominicans admitted to the United States did not report holding jobs associated with the middle class. According to INS data, most Dominicans admitted to the United States were predominantly manual and blue-collar workers, including domestic servants. In 1970 only 6.6 percent of Dominicans admitted to the United States reported being professional and technical workers, and 24.5 percent of them reported being blue-collar workers. In 1972 only 8 percent of Dominicans admitted held occupations as professional, technical, and kindred workers, but 29 percent of them were classified as operative workers. In 1977, the pattern continued, showing 6 percent of Dominicans admitted as professional, technical, and kindred workers, and 19.9 percent of them as operative workers (INS Annual Reports 1970; 1972; 1977).

Table 1 indicates that during the 1980s, the number of Dominican males classified as operators, fabricators, and laborers is 4.5 times higher than the number admitted as professionals, specialists, and technicians.

In analyzing the homes of Dominican migrants as an indication of their class status, the authors conclude that "the physical characteristics of the homes from which they come are considerably superior to those of the rest of the population. Even rural migrants tend to be better off than the rest of the rural population" (243). In the study, the comparison of migrant and nonmigrant homes showed that migrants' homes were larger, with four rooms, TV, radio, as well as other electrical goods, in-house water pipes, separate room for kitchen, and toilet with running water. Yet, what the researchers failed to identify was whether or not the social conditions found in migrants' homes, including the construction of the homes themselves, were the result of the migratory process, either via remittances or return migration. Some studies document that for many Dominican migrants, the idea of improving or buying a home in their native land is of paramount importance in their decision to emigrate. They show also that migrant homes, in contrast to nonmigrant homes, are frequently equipped with electrical and modern consumer goods imported from abroad.

In the ethnographic study of Santiago mentioned previously, Grasmuck notes that "the dream of many Dominicans when they leave for the U.S. is to work for a temporary period in order to earn enough money to buy a new home in the Dominican Republic and perhaps to start a small business upon returning"

(1985:167). She points out that several construction firms have developed in the Dominican Republic, including in the town of Santiago, to satisfy the housing demand of "Dominican-Yorkers." In contrasting migrant and nonmigrant families, Grasmuck adds that "remittances combined with the possibility of gifts from relatives living abroad mean dramatically different possibilities for obtaining consumer goods for migrant and non-migrant families" (156). She further notes that heads of migrant households had higher incomes and were more likely to have a lifestyle associated with consumer goods, including color TVs, stereos, refrigerators, and the like.

In a field study focusing on women who had emigrated in a *yola* (a small, rudimentary sailboat made of wood), conducted in 1993 in the Dominican Republic, by myself and Nancy López, we found that besides finding a job, the idea of owning or fixing up a home was a strong reason behind the decision to leave. We were further told that the physical conditions of the homes of some of the migrant women had considerably improved after migration, and that others had managed to buy a house or a piece of land to eventually build one. We noted that these migrants either fixed or built their houses in stages, taking several years to complete the project, and that its completion depended on a number of factors, ranging from the size

TABLE I **Percent Distribution of Dominican Male and Female Immigrants 16 to 64 Years Old with an Occupation (New York City, 1982–1989)**

	Male	Female
TOTAL WITH AN OCCUPATION	23,699	16,604
Professional, Specialty, and Technical	8.0	7.0
Executive, Admin., and Managerial	6.8	2.3
Sales	5.3	2.9
Administrative Support	6.2	10.3
Precision, Production, Craft, and Repair	18.3	15.8
Operator, Fabricator, and Laborer	36.6	12.9
Farming, Forestry, and Fishing	8.4	0.2
Service	10.3	48.6

SOURCE: New York City Department of City Planning 1992:83, 86.

of the home, the materials used, the kind of roofing and floor desired, the facilities involved, and, more importantly, the amount of time it took to put together the required capital. Similarly, we noted that homes where there was at least one migrant woman were equipped with a gas range, refrigerator, and electrical goods, normally a TV, radio, clock, fan, and the like (Hernández and López 1997).

From a methodological point of view, another issue that researchers who followed the 1979 socioeconomic model and who embarked in ethnographic research on migration in rural communities in the Dominican Republic failed to address was the provision of a justification for selecting a sample pool that they knew beforehand was not representative of the subject under study. If Dominican migrants are urban, as they claim, findings extracted from studies conducted in rural communities would more likely fail to provide material for inferences concerning the specificities that characterize the people who tend to migrate.

The Making of a Migratory Movement: An Alternative Reading

Our argument here is that massive migration from the Dominican Republic developed in response to the socioeconomic policies implemented in the Dominican Republic after 1966. Statistics on patterns of employment and sectoral production indicate that job loss and underemployment increased or remained high due to the developmental strategies adopted since that time. The strategies in question did not generate enough new jobs to produce an effective balance between supply and demand in the labor market. More importantly, the economic strategies tended to produce a dichotomous social order, exhibiting an impressive economic growth on the one hand and parallel growth of poverty and marginalization on the other. Specifically, the developmental models would produce a society of paradoxical and contradictory tendencies, where increasing capital accumulation would imply the use of less workers and the creation of an enlarging pool of surplus labor.

But a massive migratory movement chained primarily to one single society does not occur only through the formation and the regulation of surplus labor in the sending setting. Nor does a massive migratory movement develop based only on the wishful or rational decisions of the migrants involved. The migration of a large human contingent is a process that involves other actors besides the migrants themselves in their willingness to emigrate and the problems of that one society. It involves, for instance, the power structures of both the sending and the receiving societies, which may or may not safeguard their respective borders, may prevent or allow the migratory process, or may carry out actions and policies, which, though conceived for other pruposes, create the conditions for the movement of people from one society to another. In other words, it is unlikely that the mobility of people from one society to another could develop without the consent, either formal or informal, of the societies involved. In the case of the Dominican Republic, a parallel argument advanced here is that economic transformation entailed the complicity of the Dominican state in the stabilization of the social order by regulating surplus population via international migration and the imposition of a drastic reduction of the fertility rate.

The United States, the Rise of Balaguer, and the Circulation of Capital and Workers

During Trujillo's regime, the Dominican Republic embarked on a development strategy based primarily on the modernization of the agricultural sector, the expansion of agricultural production, and the development of an industrial complex. That model was promoted under the conviction that the Dominican Republic lacked enough people to satisfy the needs of the emerging productive market, and, therefore, emigration was severely restricted and child births were systematically encouraged. During Trujillo's reign, production was organized under the assumption that Dominicans were needed as workers and consumers to advance the economic development of the country. Consequently, any unabsorbed contingent of workers at any given moment, resulting from productive transformation, original accumulation, or economic downs, was perceived as a necessary surplus and was prevented from emigrating.

While Trujillo was in power, increases in agricultural production for both the internal and the external market, particularly during the first decade of his government, resulted from the implementation of an agrarian policy that favored the expansion of *minifundios, latifundios* (large farms), and the creation of *tierras comuneras* (communal land). Agrarian production, with the exception of sugar cane, rested mostly on the shoulders of Dominican peasants, many of whom had already lost their lands under the regime or during the North American occupation of 1916 and had been forced into a process of proletarization (Cassá 1982:118–31).

Similarly, the industrial production that developed in the urban centers, particularly in the city of Santo Domingo, depended on an available and mobile labor force. In *The Dominican Republic: A National History* Moya Pons states that "The industrialization that began during World War II and continued without interruption until 1960 altered the purely administrative character of Santo Domingo, converting it into a manufacturing center that attracted tens of thousands of Dominicans from the country and cities of the interior in search for jobs. . . . Lured by the hope of finding work in one of the new industries being built, they began to form an ample urban labor market that would supply Dominican industries with a cheap labor force in the years to come" (1995:376). Thus, the number of workers, for instance, employed in the manufacturing industry, excluding sugar, increased from 12,937 in 1950 to 18,787 in 1957, and to 24,021 in 1962 (Moya Pons 1992:378).

But if the expansion of agricultural production and the development of the industrial sector, both labor intensive productions, required an abundance of available and mobile laborers, so did the expanded bureaucracy, the construction sector, the increased army, and the new social services. While employment in the public sector increased from 40,476 in 1950 to 110,349 in 1962, total employment increased from 87,747, to 195,887 during the same years (Moya Pons 1992:378).

While Trujillo's economic strategy depended on the development of an integrated sectoral production and on intensive use of labor, President Joaquín Balaguer, his successor, implemented a strategy focused on the expansion of the industrial and commercial sectors, intensified capital investment, and the heavy use of foreign capital. These elements would alter the internal balance of Dominican society, giving rise to the formation of the socioeconomic conditions that let to the increasing mobility of people.

I

After Trujillo's death, Juan Bosch was elected president of the Dominican Republic on December 20, 1962, with over 60 percent of the popular vote. However, on September 25, 1963, after being in office for approximately seven months, Bosch's government came to an end through a military coup d'état. Collaborating in the coup were various forces of the Dominican elite, including merchants, the Catholic church, landowners, and industrialists, who did not support Bosch's candidacy, claiming that Bosch was a communist: "Bosch was replaced by a triumvirate composed of corporate executives and lawyers, and whose cabinet was made up of rightist entrepreneurs and lawyers with ties to the Dominican business community" (Moya Pons 1995:383).

After the coup d'état, the triumvirate remained in power and was supported by the church, members of the military, and the United States. With Trujillo's death, the United States increased its role in Dominican politics through President Kennedy's Alliance for Progress program, an economic aid and investment package aimed at establishing in the Latin American region governments that favored U.S. democratic policies.

It is important to note that the United States continued its direct interference into the country's political affairs until Joaquín Balaguer, a man whose politics the White House supported, became president of the Dominican Republic.

The imposed triumvirate, largely unpopular, was the target of constant civil unrest and demonstrations of social discontent, ending in a civil war headed by a number of groups, including those demanding the return of constitutionally elected President Juan Bosch. But what had began as an internal problem among Dominicans turned into an international affair when U.S. military troops invaded the Dominican Republic on April 28, 1965. "In order to stop Bosch from returning to power and 'to prevent the emergence of a second Cuba in Latin America,' U.S. President Lyndon B. Johnson ordered 42,000 U.S. soldiers to the Dominican Republic, under the pretext of saving lives and protecting U.S. interests in the country" (Moya Pons 1995:388). The military occupation would provide the grounds for the transference of influence, decisions, ideas, and resources from the United States to the occupied society.

On September 3, 1965, after an intense struggle between the Constitutionalist forces and the allied forces made up by the Dominican army and U.S. marines, the civil war ended with a signed peace treaty and the establishment of a provisional government under the watchful eyes of representatives of the Organization of the American States and the United States. Elections were scheduled for June 1966. Until then, U.S. marines remained in the country, and "the United States managed to reconstitute the Dominican military as a force directly under their command and entirely dependent on the U.S. government for the payment of salaries and the provision of clothing, food, munitions, and equipment" (Moya Pons 1995:390). As previously suggested, Joaquín Balaguer would win these elections.

II

From 1966 to 1978, the Dominican Republic, under the direction of President Joaquín Balaguer, embarked on a development project that privileged the expansion of the industrial and commercial sectors. The strategy would depend on a heavy influx of foreign capital and the promulgation of a number of economic policies favoring industrial and commercial expansion. Sociologist Wilfredo Lozano argues that government-led accumulation during the 1966–1978 period was connected to Trujillo's death, who left an incipient native bourgeoisie that, without Trujillo's tutelage, was incapable of taking a leading role to facilitate capitalist accumulation in the country (Lozano 1985:13).

It was precisely this incapacity on the part of the nascent native bourgeoisie and their commitment to further capitalist accumulation in the country that created the necessary conditions to facilitate foreign capitalist accumulation in the Dominican Republic. But also important was the need felt in the most advanced capitalist centers of the world to incorporate new lands for production, new workers, and new consumers to escape economic slow downs and unionization and, most of all, to cope with international capitalist competition, resulting from the end of World War II and the strengthening of some new countries that became new players in the capitalist world. It was a restructuring process in which both capital and workers would be constantly mobilized. It is the combination and the interplay of these factors, external and internal, that, in the end, would create the conditions in the Dominican Republic for a massive international migratory movement directed particularly toward the United States.

President Joaquín Balaguer took office on June 1, 1966, and by April 23, 1968, his government had already approved a new investment law, Law No. 299 of Industrial and Incentives Protection, which henceforward served as the basis for capitalist accumulation in the country. The approval of the new law took intense negotiations among the different factions of the Dominican bourgeoisie. The government had clearly demonstrated its commitment in facilitating the accumulation of the private sector. Yet Dominican capitalists were interested in assuring that, in spite of the entrance into the scenario of foreign capitalists, which they saw as necessary and inevitable, they would have control of specific areas of production (Moya Pons 1992:140-64).[5]

After intense negotiations, the new industrial law was finally approved. Law 299 offered a number of incentives that facili-tated industrial expansion, ranging from the removal or the reduction of tariffs to the provision of infrastructure for the development of industrial complexes. The new law also tried to prevent direct competition among foreign and national capi-talists by channeling foreign investments to new areas of production, which native capitalists could not develop. The promulgation of this law institutionalized a tripartite model of accumulation in the country constituted by the government, the private sector, and international capital. Each one depended and leaned on the other to sustain the new established social order. This collaboration would be fundamental for the devel-opment of a migratory movement to the United States.

The Politics of Stability: Family Planning and Emigration

Balaguer's political consolidation and control of the coun-try was required if the economic plan was to succeed. Consoli-dation involved a pacification of the country through political repression, killings, and incarcerations. The pacification also included expelling undesirable voices that attacked the regime, and those who represented an immediate threat to the new social order. Through an unwritten and undeclared agreement between the United States and the Dominican governments, political dissidents were granted visas and were directly dis-patched to the United States. But the magnitude of the exodus experienced by Dominican society after 1966 suggests that the opening was used not only to eliminate unwanted political dis-sidents but also other Dominicans, perhaps those whom the sys-tem had no use for.

The opening of the door for Dominicans to leave did not need an official promulgation from the government. It simply became a tacit agreement among the players. Dominicans would apply for a passport and the government would simply grant it. Contrary to Trujillo's time, virtually any one who wanted a passport could have one. Commenting on this, Frank Canelo points out that while in 1959, 19,631 people applied for a passport and only 1,805 got one, in 1969, every petition out of the 63,595 that applied received approval (1982:42). The granting of passports made concrete the opening of the door, and, through the opening of the door, emigration was tacitly encouraged by the ruling structure in the Dominican Republic.

The encouragement of emigration as a way of providing social and physical space to a society engaged in the restructuring of its social order was not new. During the 1950s, for instance, Puerto Rico witnessed the emigration of thousands of people who left a society undergoing an industrialization and modernization process. Scholars agreed that by the early 1960s, Puerto Rico enjoyed high economic growth through an impressive industrial complex based on investments from the United States. Yet, in *Labor Migration Under Capitalism: The Puerto Rican Experience* (1979), Puerto Rican scholars concluded that "without emigration, the effects of that accomplishment on living standards would have been negligible. Between 1948 and 1965 Puerto Rico saw the 'unusual spectacle of a booming economy with a shrinking labor force and . . . shrinking employment.' This seemingly paradoxical situation was made possible because migration reduced the labor force, while productivity gains were sought through an increased capital-labor ratio. . . . Estimates of the population siphoned off between 1950 and 1965 run from 900,000 to one million, including the children born abroad to migrants" (History and Migration Task Force 1979:127–28).

Although the Dominican government did not stipulate or even suggest that the emigration of people was needed to reduce population pressure, it is now clear that at the time the size of the population was a matter of concern. If the mobilization of people, unofficially encouraged, was managed in such a way that any one could simply believe that migration was the result of an individual decision rather than the result of an intended and decided political strategy on the part of the Dominican power structure, this was not the case for population control. A drastic control of population growth was firmly and clearly imposed by the Dominican State. Shortly after Balaguer took office in 1966, a National Family Planning Program was instituted. The program was integrated by the Asociación Dominicana Pro-Bienestar de la Familia (PROFAMILIA), a U.S. agency established in 1966 and financed by the American International Development Agency, and by the Consejo Nacional de Población y Familia, an official government agency created in 1968 to complement the efforts of PROFAMILIA.

The implementation of family planning (FP) in the Dominican Republic was intense. While in 1968 there were only eight clinics offering FP, by 1985 this number had increased to 493; this did not include community posts dispensing contraceptives or the services offered in private clinics under special agreement. Similarly, the number of women covered by FP increased considerably between 1975 and 1986. Among women between fifteen and forty-nine years of age, the proportion of FP users increased from 20 percent to 31 percent from 1975 to 1986; among women who were living with a man (married or not married), the proportion of users increased from 32 percent to 50 percent during the same years (Ramírez 1991:31, 34). By 1996 the number of FP centers distributed throughout the country had significantly increased to 729, and the proportion of users among married women had increased from 56 percent in 1991 to 64 percent in 1996 (*ENDESA-96*:xxvii, 6).

It is interesting to note that while a number of birth control methods are currently used in the country, including contraceptives pills, the IUD (a method no longer in use in the United States due to its association with cancer of the uterus), and Norplan (a new contraceptive used in the form of a long-acting injection and approved in the United States in 1994), permanent sterilization has increasingly become the most popular method used by women in the Dominican Republic.[6] In effect, while the use of contraceptive pills among women ranged from

5–9 percent between 1975 and 1986, sterilization dramatically increased from 8 percent to 33 percent between the same years (Tactuk et al. 1991:12). Furthermore, while the use of all methods has continued to increase, both among women and men, in the Dominican Republic sterilization has, by far, continued to be the number one method used by women to control births. Between 1991 and 1996, the use of contraceptive pills, the second most popular method among women, increased from 10 percent to 13 percent, sterilization among women increased from 39 percent to 41 percent during the same years (*ENDESA-96*:54).

In a pioneer study comparing fertility rates among Dominican women in the United States and those in the Dominican Republic, the author found that U.S. Dominican women had a higher fertility rate than women in the Dominican Republic. Among the reasons advanced by the author to explain the disparity between the two localities is the fact that removing birth control implants from their bodies may not be an easy task for women in the Dominican Republic. The author points out that "even though many clinics have a policy of providing removals regardless of the patient's ability to pay, in some cases, this information is withheld in order to prevent removal" (Outcault 2000:58). In other cases, removal is prevented simply by the difficulties encountered by many women to obtain an appointment with qualified professionals.

Statistics indicate that the implementation of FP in the Dominican Republic has been successful. After the 1960s, the fertility rate fell sharply. While in 1955, for instance, the average rate of fertility among Dominican women was close to 8 children per woman, between 1955 and 1995, this number was reduced to 3.2, placing the Dominican Republic among the four countries in Latin America with the lowest fertility rates. Between 2020 and 2025, it is expected that the fertility rate will drop further to a projected 2.6 or 1.9 children per woman, depending on whether one assumes a conservative or a more reductionist approach (Las proyecciones de población en la República Dominicana:7) (see figure 2). For the past five decades or so, major population changes in the Dominican Republic have been determined primarily by fertility rates. Consequently, the sharp decline in fertility among women has caused the population growth rate to decline from an average annual growth rate of 3.5 percent in the 1970s to 2.3 percent in the 1980s; it is projected to be 1.6% between 1990 and 2010 (*The Economist* 1990:17, 22).

The implementation of family planning in the Dominican Republic was not a conjunctural decision on the part of the United States, nor was it the result of awareness about population growth on the part of the Dominican people, as Bernardo Vega has suggested (Vega 1990:260). To the contrary, FP in the Dominican Republic was a response to long-term U.S. foreign policy on population control, particularly directed to areas that received U.S. capital investments. In his classic book *Open Veins of Latin America*, Eduardo Galeano states that "Robert McNamara, the World Bank president who was the chairman of Ford and then Secretary of Defense, has called the population explosion the greatest obstacle to progress in Latin America; the World Bank, [McNamara] says, will give priority in its loans to countries that implement birth control plans. Lyndon B. Johnson's remark,—Galeano continues—, has become famous: 'Let us act on the fact that less than $5 invested in population control is worth $100 invested in economic growth' " (Galeano 1973:15, 16). The idea was clear and simple. There were too many people in some places in the world, and their reproduction patterns were for some—particularly for those who were controlling the key to economic success and progress in the capitalist world—a social matter, an international social matter, I should say. But the message was also clear and simple. As McNamara's words suggest, participating now in the capitalist process of accumulation required, on the part of the native bourgeoisie of those countries identified with excessive population growth, the sharing of a common ideology and the willingness to allow foreigners to introduce new forms of social behaviors.

FP was first approved for Puerto Rico under the idea that there was a population excess on the island. It was believed that

population pressure on the island was the cause of extreme
poverty and high unemployment rates, which were obstacles to
socioeconomic progress. In the 1940s, on the eve of industrialization in Puerto Rico, authorities believed "that 'the pressure
of population on resources which is already great, will become
intolerably greater.' . . . At the same time that massive migration
was seen as the immediate solution, there was considerable
skepticism that the necessary volume of outward movement
could be achieved, and so education and birth control were
looked to as important additional measures" (History and
Migration Task Force 1979:120). The implementation of FP in
Puerto Rico was intense, and by 1968, while industrial production was still booming, "35 percent of the women between
twenty and forty-nine years of age had been sterilized—a proportion several times larger than the closest comparable figure
for any other country" (132).

But Puerto Rico was not alone. FP was disseminated throughout the Latin American region under the auspices of the Agency
for International Development, which from 1968 to 1972 had a
designated operating capital of $100 million. By 1986, there were
4,000 FP workers in the Dominican Republic charged with the
task of disseminating a new ideology among people. People, particularly the poor and women, were told that their poverty had to
do with their procreation of children, and that they needed to
curtail their procreation patterns. The perception of poverty as
an individual choice, rather than as a social issue, legitimized the
state of inequality in the Dominican society and exonerated the
State, the power structure, and the privileged social sectors from
distributing and sharing society's wealth. But, as outlined by
McNamara, Dominicans, after digesting the new ideology, were
now eligible for aids and loans. As it was played out in the
Dominican Republic, the adoption of FP by Dominican women
was not the result of an individual or a woman's choice. All seem
to indicate that in this country FP was an imposed social policy to
reduce population pressures.

It is important to emphasize that the United States encouraged FP in the Dominican Republic as a long-term policy to

control population growth. It is true that by 1960 the Dominican Republic had one of the highest birth rates in the region, and that anybody who believed in the so-called population explosion theory was going to be worried. But after the successful experience in Puerto Rico with FP, there should have been no doubt in the minds of U.S. representatives that population growth, either in the Dominican Republic or in any other country in the region, could be controlled through the implementation of a long-term, intense, and efficient politics of birth control, and that there was no need to suggest the implementation of other methods to undermine population pressures.

The collaboration of the U.S. and the Dominican government in the implementation of FP in the Dominican Republic clearly suggests that both perceived population growth as a problem and were interested in controlling it. The cooperation of the United States with the Dominican government in the development of the Dominican emigration, on the other hand, was the result of a conjuncture in which both agents were guided by different goals. Emigration from the Dominican Republic to the United States was encouraged by U.S. representatives as a short-term measure to eliminate an immediate problem. They saw the deportation of revolutionaries who challenged the government of Balaguer and the established new social order. The Dominican power structure, to the contrary, perceived the emigration of people not just as a temporary strategy by which political discontent could be eliminated; rather, they saw it as a long-term policy through which dissidence, as well as excess labor, could be easily eliminated.

The emigration of Dominicans to the United States was not formally discussed with the U.S. government during Balaguer's administrations. In a long newspaper article, economist Bernardo Vega, who had been the president of Banco Central from 1982 to 1984, notes that, as far as he knew, migration to the United States was never included in the agenda for discussion between the United States and the Dominican governments (Vega 1990:161). Also, in a speech given before the American Chamber of Commerce about U.S.-Dominican relations, Vega

emphasized that, from 1961 to 1982, basically two issues dominated the discussions between the United States and the
Dominican governments: the sugar quota and the amount of
aid for the Dominican Republic (Vega 1990:82). Although, as
noted by Vega, there was no discussion on the part of either governments on the issue of emigration, a door had conveniently
opened for Dominicans to emigrate to the United States. If the
United States was not interested in promoting a long-term and
massive movement of Dominicans, then the question of how the
large exodus of Dominicans to the United States developed
remains. We should begin by showing how the migration
process was initiated.

The accounts related by John Bartlow Martin in his book,
*Overtaken by Events: The Dominican Crisis from the Fall of Trujillo to
the Civil War* (1966), reveal that, as a U.S. ambassador in the
Dominican Republic, he was a key player in opening the
United States to Dominican immigration. John Bartlow Martin
had the respect of U.S. government representatives for his
knowledge about the Dominican Republic. In 1962 Martin was
appointed Ambassador of the Dominican Republic by President John F. Kennedy. He was the first appointed U.S. ambassador to the country since 1960, the year when the country was
sanctioned by the Organization of the American States, following Trujillo's failed attempt to assassinate the president of
Venezuela.

During Ambassador Martin's first official meeting with the
Consejo de Estado, a seven-member governing body, a number
of issues were discussed, including violence in Santo Domingo
and the granting of U.S. visas to Dominican troublemakers. In
his lengthy book, Martin declares that "they [the Consejo]
almost took rioting for granted—and no wonder: All last Fall
and Winter they had lived with rioting. Trujillo's fall had cut
loose long pent-up tensions, and the streets were chaotic. President Bonnelly said that well-trained Castro/Communist agents
were paying thieves and hoodlums to riot. I asked if we could
help. Reid and Bonilla Atiles immediately said yes—they
wanted technical help in training the police to control riots, in

setting up a secret anti-subversive unit to deal with Castro/Communists, and in arranging deportations" (Martin 1966:8).

But, according to Ambassador Martin, deportations had begun before his arrival in Santo Domingo in March 9 of 1962, and it seems that they had extended throughout his period: "By the end of the year [Martin says] we had some 125 deported in the United States, *most sent before I arrived. . . .* The riots mounted. Cautiously, the Consejo began to deport agitators under the Emergency Law. The Castro/Communists denounced it in the name of freedom. So did the political parties seeking the votes of the deportee' relatives. *And we became involved—we had to issue U.S. visas for people that the Consejo deported to the United States*" (99, 100; emphasis added). Furthermore, Martin claims that the Consejo wanted the United States to make sure that Dominicans deported there could not leave the country. When exactly they began deporting people is not totally clear in his book. What is clear is that during Martin's time deportation took place, and that prior to his arrival, the United States had issued visas for "Dominican communists."

But U.S. actions concerning the mobility of Dominicans to the United States did not stop with the deportations of "Castro/communists." Ambassador Martin's first trip to Washington was in April, and during his first meeting with the Secretary of State, the ambassador discussed what he classified as "the visa mess." "The visa mess" was what Ambassador Martin perceived as an increasing number of visa applicants in the Dominican Republic. Stationed daily in front of the American Consulate were long lines of people whom he believed needed to be served. In his view, the increasing number of visa applicants had created a backlog in the outdated American Consulate, and this needed to be resolved. Ambassador Martin reports in his book that "several months later," after his visit to the State Department "we finally got what we needed—a new Consulate building at the Fairgrounds, far from downtown Santo Domingo, three extra vice consuls, and a new consul" (Martin 1966:120).

Whether or not the creation of a new infrastructure and the increase of visa granting officers ended "the visa mess" in the Dominican Republic is not entirely clear. For one thing, the number of applicants has continued to increase over the years. The backlog in applications has also continued. Long lines continued to form, and all kinds of people, applicants or not, continue to wander around the American Consulate. We do know, however, that the number of U.S. immigrant visas granted in 1963 nearly tripled from 1962; the number of non-immigrant visas granted during the same year also increased considerably.

In explaining U.S. involvement in the early development of Dominican migration to the United States, Christopher Mitchell notes that "the growth in Dominican migration in these years was one of the most rapid spurts in recent population movement from any Caribbean society. The administrative simplification and speedup initiated by the U.S. Ambassador [Martin] surely contributed significantly to this high level of legal migration" (Mitchell 1992:100). The official actions taken by Martin to facilitate the migratory process, Mitchell argues, were motivated by U.S. foreign policy, which "sought (especially from 1961 to 1966) to limit political tensions in a nation where government instability was taken by Washington as an open door to radical revolution. . . . It is likely that administrative actions on migration were only loosely influenced by prevailing pro-Balaguer assumptions, rather than stemming from well-pondered choices in foreign policy" (90, 106).

As Mitchell noted, the visas granted right after Trujillo's death, that is before the civil war and Balaguer's administration, responded to a sense of fear on the part of U.S. representatives, who believed that many Dominicans were on the verge of violence. The understanding was that somehow the sense of freedom among Dominicans provided by the demise of Trujillo could lead the nation into chaos. Martin reports in his book that, while he and Sumerford (a U.S. representative stationed in the Dominican Republic) were walking in Santo Domingo in 1961 right after Trujillo's death, Sumerford referred to a number of young Dominicans who were protesting around Parque Independencia and commented: "Those boys would risk anything anywhere. They could burn the city. They'd as soon go up against the troops as not. They'd tear down the statues, set fire to the homes" (Martin 1966:68).

By enforcing peace in the Dominican Republic, U.S. officials were really trying to prevent the establishment of a social order that would deny access to U.S. capitalism in the hemisphere. Their understanding was that containment of social discontent in the Dominican Republic was a matter of life and death for capitalism in the region. That is to say that what might seem as an isolated political action on the part of the U.S. government represented, in reality, a fierce fight on the part of a socialeconomic system seeking to maintain hegemony in the region by securing its source of economic power. In the end, the prompt and opportune direct intervention of the United States into Dominican affairs was motivated by the need to kill what could have emerged, and to abort what could have represented, not just dissidence, but a totally different point of view concerning people, production, and the distribution of wealth in society.

Whether or not the fears of the U.S. government were well founded goes beyond the scope of this book. But it is important to stress that a given action, undertaken with specific and clear intentions, evolved into a process not intended nor desired by those who took the action in the first place. The reality is that U.S. representatives gave visas to Dominican troublemakers who could contest the presence of U.S. interests in the Dominican Republic. But the granting of visas would give way to the establishment of an appropriate infrastructure and logistic that would later facilitate the massive mobility of people from one society to another. From a sociological point of view, one can argue that, at the time, the manifest intention behind the United States' granting of visas was simple and clear: to eliminate political opposition. But this act would directly provoke a latent consequence—the facility for the exodus of thousands of Dominicans to the United States. The emigration of thousands of people would exonerate the Dominican state from the responsibility of providing care and services for its former citizens. The complexity of the matter comes to the fore when we regard the United States as a troubled society, where millions of people—particularly blacks and Latinos—were engaged in protests demanding an end to their discrimination and exclusion from American society.

2.

ECONOMIC GROWTH AND
SURPLUS POPULATION

During Balaguer's first two administrations, 1966–1974, the Dominican Republic witnessed impressive economic growth. Economist Miguel Ceara Hatton has characterized it as a period of "accelerated growth," reflecting a GNP annual growth rate of 12.2 percent in 1969 and 12.9 percent in 1973. During the 1969–1973 period, the manufacturing sector grew at an annual rate of 14.7 percent, construction 20.1 percent, and agriculture 8.0 ercent (Ceara Hatton 1990a:64–5). Overall, between 1970 and 1974, industrial employment grew at an annual rate of 5.9 percent (70). Most economists agree that the economic boom during Balaguer's first two terms was the result of three interconnected variables: foreign investments, foreign aid, and the high prices received for Dominican products—particularly sugar—in the international market (Ceara Hatton 1990a; Calvo and Dilla 1986). In terms of foreign-capital penetration during this period, Moya Pons concludes that "the amount of money the United States poured into the Dominican Republic between 1966 and 1973 was enormous in proportion to the small size of the country's economy" (Moya Pons 1995:397). Foreign aid, for instance, via state loans, grants, or food supplies represented approximately $122 million between 1965 and

1966, $133 million between 1967 and 1969, and $78 million per year between 1969 and 1973. Direct foreign investments, on the other hand, increased from $154 million in 1964 to $396 in 1972, of which about 89 percent represented direct investment from the United States (Del Castillo et al. 1974:183).

But what is still missing in the analysis of economic growth is the role that State demographic control, via the institutionalization of the international mobility of people and the contraction of the natural growth of the population, played in the viability of the reorganization of production and the stabilization of Dominican society. The Puerto Rican experience seems to indicate that it is unlikely that a capitalist economic project based on foreign investments tending to reduce the use of labor would have reached any level of success in the Dominican Republic, if the hundreds of thousands of men and women who were put into motion—whether formally or informally—had remained and the birth rate had not been severely reduced.

The Road to Modernization: Import Substitution

Since 1966, the Dominican Republic, in seeking to modernize and develop the country as well as to compete effectively in the international market, has adopted a number of economic strategies. The first strategy, Import Substitution (IS), had been initiated by Trujillo during the 1950s, and Balaguer's government, through Law 299, passed during his second year in power, formalized a new version of the economic strategy. IS was based on the theories of economist Raul Prebisch, who believed that underdeveloped countries could accomplish a capitalist national development by implementing import substitution, that is, by limiting the level of imports and by developing an industrial infrastructure for assembling or manufacture of similar goods within the country. In keeping with the ideas proposed by Prebisch, IS's emphasis on industrial accumulation generated a rapid expansion of the industrial sector in the Dominican Republic. Between 1970 and 1974, industrial production grew at an annual rate of 120 percent

(Duarte and Corten 1982). Between 1970 and 1977, the capital invested in the food industry increased from DR$130.9 million to DR$196.8 million, and in the intermediary industry, from DR$31.2 million to DR$70.5 million (Vicens 1982).

But industrial expansion and increase in production occurred within contradictory tendencies, generating an involutionary process that affected the entire process of accumulation. Industrial production depended heavily on the importation of foreign materials and technology, as well as on State subsidies, and it failed to diversify the infrastructure. The creation of new jobs was also affected by the increased use of technology and by the adoption of technology over human labor in the process of production. In the end, these tendencies imposed limitations on the level of accumulation associated with the native bourgeoisie, aggravated the unemployment and underemployment problem, and, ultimately, created a structurally disarticulated economy.

While in 1970 total imports of foreign inputs, excluding the sugar industries, represented 24.5 percent, by 1977 total industrial imports had increased to 38.8 percent (Vicens 1982:136). The small group of industries engaged in the manufacturing of intermediary and heavy products alone demanded up to three quarters of foreign inputs during the same years (Ceara Hatton 1986:96). As a direct consequence, the flight of capital from the Dominican Republic toward the industrialized countries, particularly the United States, increased from DR$78.9 million in 1970 to DR$388.8 million in 1977 (Vicens 1982:138).

The tendency to import foreign inputs, from technology to raw materials for industrial production, led into a lack of industrial and sectoral integration. In effect, while 85 percent of the manufacturing industry emphasized the production of nondurable goods that required low levels of industrial transformation, particularly food and garments, only 12 percent and 3 percent, respectively, of the industrial capacity was dedicated to the production of intermediary and capital-related goods, particularly goods for the construction industry. Similarly, although

the country had the resources to grow tobacco for the production of cigarettes, using the exemptions provided by Law 299,
manufacturers imported tobacco to be processed in the country, thereby contributing to the Dominican economy's lack of
sectoral integration.

In a 1973 speech, President Balaguer, justifying the subsidies given by the State to private industrial developers in the
country, stated that "in 1972, the government granted a total of
DR$60,621,333.86 in exonerations to the private industrial sec-
tor. Without any doubt, this is a tremendous sacrifice on the
part of the State, which is badly in need of fiscal resources to
invest in the country's urgently needed construction. But this is
the price that we must pay to develop the country and, within a
few years, be able to have an industrial development capable of
not only substituting many of the imports demanded today, but
also capable of absorbing a great deal of our unemployed workers" [author's translation].[1]

But contrary to President Balaguer's predictions, IS failed
these purposes miserably. It did not substitute imports, nor did
it reduce unemployment levels. Imports of consumer-related
manufactured products increased in almost every industrial
branch. From 1973 to 1980, imports of total manufactured
products, for instance, increased from 26.8 percent to 31.9 percent. Similarly, while the importation of food, tobacco, and bev-
erages also increased during the same years, from 7.5 percent to
9.8 percent, furniture increased from 4.78 percent to 12.41 percent, clothing from 13.48 percent to 22.76 percent, shoes from
4.26 percent to 10.62 percent, and paper from 31.32 percent to
49.40 percent (Ceara Hatton 1990a:80–81).

In 1970, when unemployment data were first officially
recorded in the country, the national population census reported
an unemployment rate of 24.1 percent. Table 2.1 indicates that
since then, the rate of unemployment has remained considerably
high throughout the years. Although industrial production was
highly concentrated, particularly in the city of Santo Domingo,
which contained over two thirds of the country's industries, by
1973, the unemployment rate in this city was 20 percent.

Between 1970 and 1979, 305,600 men and women entered the labor force. But during the same years, the total number of employed workers in the industrial sector increased from 113,040 to 139,503, an absolute increase of 26,463 jobs in a period of nine years, an average of less than 3,000 new jobs created per year. Industrial employment is also undermined by ups and downs in the economy. From 1987 to 1993, for instance, pressured by the severe economic crisis of the 1980s, the industrial sector significantly reduced its number of workers, from 164,000 to 143,000 (Ramirez 1999:11). Thus, contrary to Balaguer's views, the direct transference of resources from the State to the private sector—formally expressed through Law 299—did not significantly alter the internal structure of the industrial sector by expanding its needs to incorporate new workers into the process of industrial production.

The constant increase of technology over labor in the process of industrial production tended to negatively affect the elasticity

TABLE 2.1 **Unemployment Rates** (*Percentage of labor force*)

Year	(%)
1970	24.1
1973*	20.0
1978*	24.4
1979*	19.3
1980	22.2
1981	20.7
1982	21.3
1983	22.1
1984	24.2
1985	27.2
1986	28.7
1987	25.0
1988	20.8
1989	19.6
1990	19.7
1991	26.6

*Santo Domingo

SOURCES: For 1970–1979, Ceara Hatton 1990b:60; for 1980–1991, Ceara Hatton and Croes Hernández 1993:18.

of demand in the industrial sector. While in 1960, for instance, the creation of an industrial job required DR$3,125, by 1968 the required capital had increased to DR$5,000, and by 1981 to more than DR$9,000. Moya Pons has argued that critics of Law 299, when calculating the amount of capital required to create a new job, failed to include the contributions of the State into the creation of the job. He points that "between 1972 and 1980, only 28,049 direct jobs were created under the incentives offered by Law 299, and the State contributed to the creation of these jobs with DR$139.7 million of uncollected taxes. . . . The State contributed with an average of DR$6,582 in every new job created during this period" (Moya Pons 1992:346; author's translation).

Similarly, between 1968 and 1981, a total of 678 new industries were approved under Law 299. These industries, holding an investment capital of DR$498,664, created only 54,891 new jobs, an average of 4,222 jobs per year. By 1981 industrial expansion still demanded fewer than 5,000 new workers per year at a time when the active economic population was growing at an annual rate of 5.5 percent each year, generating some 56,000 working-aged men and women.

Critics of the IS model have also argued that the emphasis placed on industrial expansion did not significantly alter the level of industrialization in the country. From 1969 to 1973, for instance, the level of industrialization increased from 14.8 percent to 18.6 percent (Ceara Hatton 1990a:72). In the early 1970s, however, the level of industrialization declined, undergoing a loss of little more than a single percentage point between 1974 and 1984, when it decreased from 18.4 percent to 17.2 percent (Ceara Hatton 1986:132).

The Cattle-Agricultural Sector

The emphasis placed on industrial expansion had an adverse effect on the development of the agriculture-ranching sector, whose contribution to the GNP would decrease progressively. *Latifundismo*, as well as the intensification of capital in the agribusiness industry, affected the development of jobs in the countryside, provoking unemployment and an increasing mobilization to urban centers.

The agrarian sector is characterized by profound and severe contradictions reflected in the unequal distribution of land and the emphasis on producing for an export market based on the underutilization of land and workers. From 1971 to 1981, the absolute number of *latifundios* of 16,000 *tareas*[2] or more decreased from 216 to 161, but their average size increased from 46,538 to 59,474 *tareas*, reflecting a higher concentration of arable land. By 1981 only 1.83 percent of landowners holding *latifundios* of 800 *tareas* or more occupied more than half of all the arable land in the country, equivalent to 55.23 percent.

The National Agrarian Census showed that there were 185,292 small farms in 1971, each holding between eight and seventy-nine *tareas*, with an average size of twenty-nine *tareas*, occupying just 12.47 percent of the arable land. By 1981, however, the distribution reflected a higher fragmentation of land among small landowners. The number of farms, for instance, holding between eight and seventy-nine *tareas* increased from 185,292 to 252,995, but the proportion of the area occupied by these farms decreased from 12.47 percent to 11.71 percent, with the average size of the farm also declining from twenty-nine to twenty *tareas*.[3]

Traditionally, *latifundios* have required a small number of Dominican workers. Take, for instance, the activities of cattle-raising and sugarcane. Cattle-raising concentrates the largest amount of land and does not require much labor, for animals do not need much special attention. More importantly, cattle-raising is extensive, and landowners tend to use between ten and fifteen *tareas* per head of live stock. Sugarcane represents the second largest production in the *latifundios*. But this production is seasonal and has been organized around the use of Haitian labor, a cheaper labor force, eliminating the need to incorporate Dominican workers into the process of sugar production.

Small farms produce food for internal consumption, using approximately 29 percent of the available land, and producing

over 40 percent of the food on farms consisting of less than
eighty *tareas*. The small proportion of land allocated to produce
for local consumption—its increasing fragmentation, the use of
obsolete methods of production, and, most of all, the lack of
available resources for agricultural production (capital, technology, and other inputs)—have created a growing shortfall in
the production of food products for local consumption. This
shortfall is filled by increasing food imports.

By the 1970s, it was evident that the agrarian subsector faced
a structural crisis, as reflected in its inability to satisfy the
demand of the internal market. Production in the sector slowed
down progressively, decreasing from an average rate of growth
of 4.1 percent in 1966 to 1.29 percent in 1981, reaching negative
rates of growth in 1984 and 1985, of -0.9 percent and -3.9 percent respectively (Ceara Hatton 1986:46). Imports of food for
local consumption slowly replaced the need to improve internal
production, contributing to the displacement of workers.

Thus, from virtual self-sufficiency in food production in the
1950s, the Dominican Republic fell into a pattern of having to
import increasing amounts of basic foodstuff, including rice,
fish, oil, meat, vegetables, eggs, milk, and grains. Imports of
food products increased from $43 million in 1972 to $230 million in the 1980/1981 period (Ceara Hatton 1986:51). Table 2.2

TABLE 2.2 **Import of Products in 1990 (*In millions of DR$*)**

Products	$
Rice	29.2
Sunflower Oil	15.5
Beans	60.9
Cotton Oil	23.5
Milk	36.8
Soy Oil	233.5
Garlic	5.8
Potatoes	2.0
Onion	4.3
Spaghetti	3.3
Pork Meat	1.8

SOURCE: D'Oleo 1991:56.

shows that in 1990 the Dominican Republic imported a total of DR\$415.4 million in basic food products, DR\$69.9 million more than in 1989 (D'Oleo Ramírez 1991:55). On the other hand, increasing importation, scarcity, and commercial speculation in the market led to a progressive increase in the price of food, reaching a 31 percent increase from 1980 to 1984. The disparity between prices, particularly of food products, and low salaries gave way to a severe inflation, contracting the real value of the *peso* to \$0.30 in 1980. In effect, while in 1980 the monthly average cost for feeding a family of six was DR\$162.00, the minimum wage salary stood at DR\$125.00, representing a gap of DR\$37.00. By 1984, however, after a minimum wage increase from DR\$125.00 to DR\$175.00, the gap slightly expanded when the monthly average cost for food increased to DR\$213.50, exceeding the minimum wage by DR\$38.50 per month.

Even when growers were successful in increasing the production of basic foods, such as rice, beans, tomato, onion, and garlic, in response to the implementation of government-led programs, particularly after 1978, prices for these products remained unreachable for most people. Domestic growers not only continued to use foreign inputs for their cultivation, but their output was not large enough to produce a significant change in the size of the supply.

A recent study by the International Labor Organization (ILO) among six countries in Central America and the Dominican Republic found that among the countries compared, the cities of Santo Domingo, in the Dominican Republic, and Panamá, in Panamá, had the highest monthly prices for a Basic Food Basket (BFB) for a family of four, or \$236 and \$219 respectively. The same study reports that in the Dominican Republic, a monthly industrial minimum salary buys only three fourths of a BFB (Del Cid and Chen 1999:31).

The agrarian-ranching sector progressively reduced its need to use labor, undermining the creation of jobs in the countryside. In effect, from 1960 to 1970, the absolute number of people employed in the agricultural-ranching sector decreased from 1,118,000 to 723,000 (Ramírez et al. 1982:20). By 1980 this number had decreased to 691,000 (Santana and Tatis 1985:9), and by 1991 to 458,000 (Ramírez 1999:10). (See figure 8). As a direct result, unemployment in the area remained high, over 20 percent, even when the economy experienced unprecedented growth. The rural unemployment rate increased from 24.2 percent in 1970 to 26.1 percent in 1980, decreased to 22.8 percent in 1981, and rose again to 25.5 percent in 1984. By 1991 *ENDESA-91* reported an unemployment rate of 24.2 percent in rural areas. Underemployment, on the other hand, increased in rural areas from 40 percent% in 1973 to 42 percent by 1980.[4]

Urban Centers and the Mobility of Surplus Labor

The inability of the agriculture-ranching sector to absorb the increasing population of workers provoked the movement of people from the countryside to urban centers. Between 1950 and 1980, the Dominican Republic witnessed impressive urban growth, particularly from 1960 to 1970. From 1920 to 1950, the proportion of urban people in the Dominican Republic increased from 16.6 percent to 23.8 percent. By 1981 this percentage had more than doubled, increasing to 52.0 percent, and by 1985 to 57.7 percent. In 1950 only Santo Domingo and Santiago had 20,000 or more people, but by 1960 five other towns reached that level of population. By 1970 the number of cities with a populated of 20,000 or more people had already increased to fifteen.

It is estimated that between 1960 and 1970, 389,288 people migrated from rural areas, particularly from the Cibao region, into urban centers. Between 1970 and 1980, the number of migrants increased to 536,054 (Ariza Castillo et al. 1991:76). It is interesting to note that after 1960, more than 70 percent of the migrants were attracted to the Southeast, a region where industrial capital began to develop during the first administrations of Balaguer. The movement of people from the countryside to the cities in pursuit of jobs suggests that rapid urbanization in the country is the result of a landless peasantry rendered unable to reproduce itself in the countryside through a process of proletarianization.

Unfortunately for many Dominicans, the urban centers also had their own problems. Many of the urban areas were not prepared to absorb and accommodate the increasing number of people who arrived seeking employment. It was not only the jobs that were lacking, but for many of those who managed to get jobs, the pay was low and the conditions were bad. For many movers, urbanization simply implied a change in their spatial distribution, but not a transformation of their social life or their occupations. Many "urban" Dominicans lacked running and drinkable water, a sewage system, paved streets, housing facilities, schools, health-care centers, and, most of all, access to communication with the rest of the city where they lived. Migration led to high concentrations of people in established urban areas and contributed to the demographic expansion of such areas. But people's arrival and settlements emphasized the state of inequality existing in the urban spaces. Urbanization reflected a class society clearly marked by the housing patterns and the distribution of spaces, as well as by the goods and services available in the city.

Take, for instance, the case of Santo Domingo, the most populated and modern city in the Deminican Republic, and which attracted the most migrants. Census data indicated that in 1970 65 percent of the heads of the households in Santo Domingo were immigrants, and that 89 percent of the nation's total migrants selected this city as their point of destination. Dominican demographers claim that this city alone absorbed 47 percent of the country's urban growth for the past sixty-five years. Similarly, by 1980 Santo Domingo accounted for 73.2 percent of all of the country's wholesalers; had 71.8 percent of construction permits, 74.5 percent of telephones, and 75 percent of automobiles. Between 1977 and 1987, the number of registered supermarkets in Santo Domingo increased from 91 to 225, travel agencies from 165 to 404, credit-card agencies from 3 to 21, and computer centers from 11 to 78. But this city, where between 1963 and 1982, the amount of invested capital was multiplied by five and the number of tourists increased twenty times, is also the most concrete expression of the contradictions of a capitalist urban setting.

The many poor *barrios* (neighborhoods) that have developed in the city of Santo Domingo within the past thirty years have resulted from direct migration rather than from natural population increase. The majority of the people who move to the city reside in popular and marginal *barrios*.[5] It is estimated that the population of these areas represents 81 percent of the city's households. Yet they occupy only 39.5 percent of its physical space (Cela, Duarte, and Gómez 1988:21). These crowded *barrios* represent the concrete limits of modernity and urban expansion in this city. For instance, as many as 2,900 school-aged children had no seats in the only existing public school in the *barrio* Los Guandules, and 26.2 percent of poor people residing in *barrios* located north of the city had no running water in their houses, and as many as half of them have never seen a garbage pick-up truck in their area (Cela, Duarte, and Gómez 1988:8).

In an ethnographic study conducted in five poor *barrios* of Santo Domingo during 1976 and 1977, sociologist Isis Duarte found that more than 90 percent of the residents of these *barrios* were immigrants, and that, as the researchers expected, more than 54 percent of them had migrated from rural parts of the country, particularly from the Cibao region (Duarte 1980:223). This study, the largest and most detailed survey to date concerning working people in poor neighborhoods, revealed that the majority of the workers had service-sector jobs and that more than 66 percent of the heads of households engaged in the labor force belonged to the relative surplus population. These workers earned between DR$0.00 and less than DR$4.00 per day at the time of the survey (286).

The study found that unemployment in the *barrios* represented 16.3 percent of the labor force, a lower rate than the official rate for the city, which stood at more than 20 percent for almost the entire decade. They concluded, however, that in reality the rate of unemployment was much higher in the *bar-*

rios, since 10 percent of those who had jobs had not earned any wage during the reference week selected in the survey, which clearly represented hidden unemployment (295). Similarly, of those who were currently working, only 35.2 percent had permanent jobs. A solid 61 percent of them had been temporarily laid off at some time during their most recent job, and only 20 percent had been able to find a second job to complement their inadequate earnings (413).

It is interesting to note in this study that neither the number of years living in the city nor the amount of time performing the same job helped to improve the migrants' outcomes in the labor market. Although education was found to correlate strongly with workers' stability in the labor market, its effect on earnings and occupation was less significant. The higher percentage of workers with nine years of education or more was found among those holding jobs in community service (office, military, teachers, and kindred), representing 48.7 percent. But while an overwhelming 94.1 percent of these workers held permanent positions, only 62 percent of them earned enough to reproduce their labor power (DR$4.00 or more per day), and the majority of them had learned their skills on the job (287).

Economic Rearticulation in Search of Accumulation

"El que paga la música, escoge el son" (who pays
for the music chooses the tune).
—*Popular saying.*

By the mid-1970s, the Dominican Republic had shifted from production that was mainly oriented to traditional products (coffee, sugar, tobacco, and cocoa) to production oriented to the development of free-trade zones (FTZ), tourism, and the cultivation of nontraditional agrarian products. The demand for traditional Dominican agrarian products began to fall in the international market, particularly in the United States, as the demand for other goods rose. For example, while

the contribution of sugar to the GNP, whose production constituted the base of the Dominican economy, was reduced from
an average of 25 percent during the last years of the 1970s to
about 8 percent in 1990, tourism accounted for more than 40
percent of GNP by the end of the 1980s. Although these
changes began to manifest themselves clearly during the
1980s, when the contribution of these sectors to the GNP
increased significantly, the reality is that the shift in production
was already in the making during Balaguer's first administration through his open-door policy to foreign investments.

Critics have argued that capitalist accumulation via foreign
investment tends to deform and subordinate the local economy
to outside forces. In *Reformismo Dependiente* (1985), sociologist
Wilfredo Lozano argues that foreign loans in particular presuppose a series of commitments toward lending institutions,
and that they serve as a vehicle to intensify the dependency of
the Dominican Republic. He states that "these commitments do
not only imply the direct payment to cover the loan but also a
number of measures related to economic development, subordinated to specific strategies designed by the international
agencies and the binding of the Dominican import market to
the supply of goods produced by the lending countries"
(Lozano 1985:187, 189; author's translation). Others emphasize that foreign capital does not contribute to the diversification of the local economy, since it is normally directed to target
areas of production for which an international market already
exists (Del Castillo et al. 1974).

As argued by Lozano, the effects of foreign investment have
been felt on the supply side of the market, which has increasingly become flooded with goods produced in the United
States. A recent article shows, for instance, that the same U.S.
products when sold in the Dominican market had much higher
prices than in the U.S. market. In comparing the cost of basic
supermarket products, the author establishes that the same
U.S. products cost between three and five times more in the
Dominican market than in the United States (Riley de Dauhajre 1995:1). (See figures 3A–C). It is important to emphasize

that the importation of these products created a new market and new consumers, which directly contributed to the expansion of both international and native capitalist accumulation. Thus, while Dominican consumers are forced to pay higher prices, the mobility of goods and the new demands associated with it contribute to the expansion of U.S. industrial capital and native capital associated with commercial and import sectors.

Foreign investments, or the relocation of capital, responded to a reorganization of production in advanced capitalist societies seeking to further the process of accumulation. The reorganization involved the relocation of capital and production, or the shipping away from its original base, particularly off-shore, of as many aspects of the process of production as possible. The basic aim behind the move was the reduction of the cost of production to further the accumulation of capital. But the relocation of production did not imply the loss of the markets these goods already had before the move. Quite to the contrary, the relocation created new markets, but it kept the old ones that were also glutted with imported goods. During the 1980s, under the administration of President Ronald Reagan, the Agency for International Development (AID) further emphasized the relocation of capital and production outside the boundaries of the United States. AID was charged with the mission of producing projects that would encourage U.S. investments outside the United States. The agency's bilateral loans were targeted at countries that strongly encouraged the development of private projects dealing with the production of light manufacturing and, in agriculture, the production of nontraditional products.

While the move of U.S. capitalists was financially supported through the agency's Overseas Private Investment Corporation, in 1981 AID created the Bureau of Private Enterprise to sponsor the creation of partnerships between the United States and native capitalists in projects related to the agribusiness industry. In President Salvador Jorge Blanco's 1982 letter of intention to the International Monetary Fund (IMF), it was agreed that part of the $466.5 million lent by the IMF to the Dominican Republic was going to be used in economic activities capable of increasing the level of investments in the country, from 19.5 percent in 1982 to 22.5 percent in 1985. The imposition of international capitalism over the internal productive structure of the Dominican Republic is clearly perceived when one notes that after 1982, economic activities encouraged by the government in the private sector were precisely those connected to foreign capitalists, including collaborative projects between native and foreign capital, such as manufacture, agribusiness, and tourism (Ceara Hatton 1990a:160).

The development of FTZ during the 1970s and the cultivation of nontraditional agricultural products in the agribusiness industry during the 1980s in the Dominican Republic are productive modalities that responded directly to this new pattern of accumulation. Both modalities are interconnected with the relocation of capital and production and the entrance of foreign capital into the country after 1966. Some have read these as a strategy whereby smart Dominican capitalists who, affected by protectionist barriers, lost their niche in the international market and sought new ways to accumulate wealth. But it would seem, rather, that for the Dominican bourgeoisie, the shift reflected the true nature of a dependent capitalist accumulation process, that is, their subordinated position in the capitalist order. The shift in production was orchestrated by enterprises such as the American company Dole, whose owners were convinced that they could no longer compete effectively in the world market and that they needed to relocate the production of pineapples from Hawaii to the Dominican Republic. Those who owned Dole believed that the loss of their company's competitiveness (lower profits, that is) had to do with workers, the pickers, who by 1990, after sixty-nine long years of picking pineapples in Hawaii, were earning as much as $8.23 an hour, while competitors were paying workers much less in Thailand and the Philippines. To the owners of Dole, the move was imperative.

Since 1969, attracted mainly by the high number of unemployed people, low wages, and, most of all, the fiscal incentives provided by the Dominican government—including high tax exemptions and a favorable monetary exchange rate—foreign capitalists began to invest in the first free-trade zones in the Dominican Republic. The first free-trade zone, with just one industry in operation, opened in the eastern part of the country, in a town called La Romana, but by 1988 there were sixteen free-trade zones distributed throughout the country, with 224 industrial installations. The number of direct jobs created increased from 504 to 85,000.

The establishment of industries in the free-trade zones really intensified during the 1980s, particularly after 1985, when the number of new factories jumped from 71 to 136, and the number of direct jobs increased from 16,440 to 30,902. By 1993 there were 462 industrial plants and 164,296 direct jobs operating in thirty free-trade zones. (See table 2.3). By 1988, after México, the Dominican Republic had the largest number of industrial installations in free-trade zones in the Latin American and Caribbean region (Abreu et al. 1989:68). But critics agreed that although free-trade zones have generated badly needed jobs and revenues, they have not contributed significantly to the industrial development of the country nor alleviated its unemployment problem.

From a macroeconomic point of view, critics question the contribution of free-trade zones to the development and expansion of industrial production in the country. They believe that free-trade zones have emphasized the disconnection between sectorial production by continuing to import most of its industrial inputs, and by having industries that are engaged in the final stage of the production process, eliminating the need to develop transformative industries. In other words, these are not industries that help to industrialize the country. They also find that free-trade zones operate as economic enclaves, whose only connection with the country's economy is the wages paid to workers and the revenues generated for the use of the infrastructure (Ceara Hatton 1986; 1990b; Duarte 1986).

From a labor-market point of view, critics have argued that industrial employment represented approximately 13 percent of the country's labor force, but free-trade zones only employed

3 percent of them. By 1996 free-trade zones, after thirty years of
operation in the country and a significant increase in the number of industries, managed to employ no more than 5 percent
of the Dominican people (*ENDESA-96:2*).

Likewise, most free trade-zone workers are women migrants,
have very low levels of unionization, and earn less than the minimum established wage in the country (Gómez 1988). It has also
been argued that the recruitment of young women as the primary source of employment and the high rate of turnover in
free trade-zone plants have contributed to increased levels of
unemployment among women (Sassen 1988:97).

One could safely argue that the emphasis placed in recruit-
ing young women for production contributes to expanding the
absolute size of the labor force and undermines the possibilities
of free-trade zones as a solution to the growing unemployment
problem. The composition by sex of the active population of
workers in the Dominican Republic clearly reflects a tendency
toward the "feminization" of the labor force. In 1960 for every
100 persons engaged in the labor force, 11 were women, but by
1981, this number had increased to 29, and by 1983, in the city
of Santo Domingo, which has a large population of incoming
migrants, the number rose to 38. The growing proletarization
of women is associated with the expansion of the manufacturing sector, particularly free-trade zones, where they made considerable gains, jumping from 17.5 percent in 1960 to 28.1 percent in 1981 (Báez 1985).

TABLE 2.3 **Evolution of FTZ in the Dominican Republic**

Year	1975	1980	1985	1990	1993	1996
# of FTZ	3	3	8	25	30	32
Industries	29	71	136	331	462	476
Jobs	5,872	16,440	30,902	130,045	164,296	176,000
Revenues in million US$	12.8	44.5	54.6	214.0	350.0	—*

*Not available.

SOURCES: For 1975–1993, Manzueta Martinez 1994; for 1996, *ENDESA-96* 1996:2.

Tourism has undergone remarkable growth during the past fifteen years. The amount of revenue generated by this subsector jumped from $16.4 million in 1970 to $616 in 1988, becoming the single largest contributor to the national economy. From 1980 to 1988, the number of hotel rooms more than doubled, increasing from 5,394 to 13,451, and the number of incoming tourists increased from 753,000 in 1985 to more than 1 million in 1987 (Ceara Hatton 1990b:4–5). Compared to 1988, the number of hotel rooms in the country had nearly tripled by 1996.

In spite of the remarkable expansion, the tourist industry represents a volatile, seasonal, and highly competitive economic activity that depends on tourists' financial ability, time, and interest in visiting the Dominican Republic. Similarly, its multiplying effects on the economy is highly limited. The service it renders is consumed right at the time of "production" and does not give room for resale. At the same time, the tourist industry helps to increase the level of importation in the country. This economic activity imports most of the products it uses, from the beds, linen, and silverware to most of the food tourists consume. But, most of all, tourism is a capital intensive activity that functions on the basis of a skilled and semiskilled labor force, providing very little room for the employment of unskilled workers. In effect, although tourism generates the largest amount of revenue in the GNP since early 1980, the number of jobs generated in this area has shown only a modest increase, from 10,800 in 1980 to 17,258 in 1987, and to 24,000 in 1989. By 1996 the number of direct jobs generated by the tourist industry had increased to 35,000 (*ENDESA-96*:2)

The Reproduction of Labor Power and Surplus Labor: The Antecedent to Emigration

Theoretically, besides being direct producers, workers are also consumers whose salaries help expand the process of accumulation. In advanced capitalist societies, the remuneration of workers is linked to their internal process of capital accumulation. In these countries, low wages and long periods of unemployment are generally subsidized by the government, through some kind of welfare system or massive construction projects, as an indirect way of stimulating and generating consumption internally. The history of the evolution of wages in the Dominican Republic shows that, contrary to advanced technological societies, the remuneration has been traditionally perceived by capitalists as an expenditure rather than as a possible source of accumulation. Capitalists in this country, seeking to reduce costs in the process of production, constantly undermine the cost of labor.

Some authors have argued that the existence of low wages in Latin America is related to the fact that these countries' economies are oriented to the export market, and capitalist accumulation is divorced from the process of circulation (buying, selling, and consumption). Capitalist accumulation depends mainly on the extraction of surplus value through the overexploitation of workers, or on the reduction of their wages to a level incapable of reproducing the worker's own labor power. What makes the process of overexploitation possible is the large supply of workers in relation to a reduced demand in Latin America (Marini 1973).

Low wages limit worker consumption in the internal market, but the lower remuneration of workers' value, or super exploitation, bespeaks workers' inability to reproduce their labor power. The reproduction of a worker's labor power is a process which, as described by Claude Meillassoux in *Maidens, Meal, and Money* (1981), goes beyond one worker involved in production. Meillassoux explains that "the volume of subsistence goods produced by each producer must equal or surpass the amount needed to maintain the producer himself, to bring up future producers, and to service the retirement of those who are no longer producing" (1981:51–2). While future producers represent the worker's replacement in the labor force, retired producers represent those who, at the time the worker was underage, provided his reproduction. The reproduction of the three constitutes the reproduction of the worker.

The wage structure in the Dominican Republic generates both processes: a reduced internal market disconnected from most workers' consumption and the workers inability to reproduce their labor power. In the case of free-trade zones, for instance, their comparative advantage is based on paying extremely low wages in the Dominican Republic. At the time when the first free-trade zone was established, salary was set 20 percent below the country's official minimum wage, which at the time was DR$60.00 per month. But, as early as 1971, inflationary prices progressively began to reduce the value of the nominal salary, pushing down its real value. After several increases, nominal salary increased from DR$60.00 in 1969 to DR$400.00 per month in 1988. But during the same years, the real value of the salary declined progressively, falling from a base value of DR$60.00 to DR$36.00. (See table 2.4.)

Similarly, workers' low earnings impact on their standard of living. In 1981 the nominal salary was DR$125.00 per month, but Duarte, Corten, and Pou estimated that during the same year, workers needed DR$181.00 to buy the basic goods and services they used to buy in 1969 with DR$60.00 (1986:139). By 1982 the gap between earnings and the price of basic goods widened. The nominal salary had remained constant at DR$125.00, but the price of basic goods and services had increased to DR$279.50, excluding any expense related to family entertainment (Vicens 1982:326).

In *Capitalismo y Super Población en Santo Domingo: Mercado de Trabajo Rural y Ejército de Reserva Urbano*, Duarte argues that "the mechanisms of super exploitation deny workers the necessary conditions to reconstitute their energy. By preventing workers from consuming even what is essential to restore their own energy, workers are condemned to a premature exhaustion" (Duarte 1980:67–8; author's translation). Duarte also stresses that overexploitation results from the availability of an abundant working population, generated by a given process of production. She adds that "migrations represent a mechanism of redistributing that surplus population. The emigration zones, or the areas where the population is rejected, are areas where

TABLE 2.4 **Inflation, Minimum Nominal, and Real Salary (*Monthly DR$*)**

Year	CPI (base 1970)	Inflation (%)	Nominal Salary	Real Salary	R.S. Index
1970	1.000	0.00	60	60	1.000
1971	1.043	4.30	60	58	0.967
1972	1.125	7.86	60	53	0.883
1973	1.295	15.11	60	46	0.767
1974	1.465	13.12	60	41	0.683
1975	1.677	14.47	90	54	0.900
1976	1.809	7.87	90	50	0.833
1977	2.041	12.82	90	44	0.733
1978	2.186	7.10	90	41	0.683
1979	2.386	9.15	125	52	0.867
1980	2.785	16.72	125	45	0.750
1981	2.995	7.54	125	42	0.700
1982	3.224	7.65	125	39	0.650
1983	3.447	6.92	125	36	0.600
1984[10]	4.290	24.46	158	37	0.617
1985[11]	5.89	937.51	213	36	0.600
1986	6.474	9.75	250	39	0.650
1987[12]	7.503	15.89	283	38	0.633
1988[13]	11.029	46.99	385	35	0.583

Formulas: Real Salary: 3/1 = 4
Real Salary Index: 4/3 1970 = 5
Rate of Inflation: $\dfrac{Old\ CPI - New\ CPI \times 100}{Old\ CPI} = 2$

[10] Increased to DR $175 in May.
[11] Increased to DR $250 in July.
[12] Increased to DR $350 in September.
[13] Increased to Dr $400 in June for the private sector and in April for the public sector.
  SOURCE: Adapted from Ceara Hatton 1990b:75.

the productive forces are incapable of absorbing the growing surplus population" (75; author's translation).

Economic Accumulation and Crisis

Since the end of the 1960s, in seeking to integrate itself into the world economy, the Dominican Republic has implemented two development strategies: import substitution and the export-led economy. The first emphasized industrial production, which, among other things, was intended to reduce the level of importation of manufactured products. But, as critics argued, the model failed in its essential mandate. By 1978 it was obvious that the country was importing much more than it was producing and selling. Consequently, a growing deficit began to characterize the economy (see table 2.5), and an increasing amount of money was borrowed from foreign institutions. In the beginning, money was borrowed mostly to pay for food, oil, capital goods, and industrial inputs, but later, money was also borrowed to pay for public expenditure and the interests accrued on the same debt. Thus, from a foreign debt of $290.6 million in 1970, by 1988 the debt had reached the phenomenal sum of $3.84 billion.

But it was even worse than that. As explained previously, by the end of the 1980s, the Dominican economy had essentially the same industrial coefficient it had in 1968, when Law 299 of the industrial incentives was approved. But if the level of industrialization had not increased, the same could not be said about the intensification of capital in the industrial setting, which by

TABLE 2.5 **Foreign Trade (*In millions of US$*)**

Year	Export	Import	Balance
1977	780	847	-67
1978	676	860	-184
1979	869	1,080	-211
1980	962	1,498	-536
1981	1,188	1,450	-262
1982	768	1,248	-480
1983	785	1,279	-494
1984	868	1,257	-389
1985	739	1,286	-547
1986	722	1,266	-544
1987	711	1,591	-880
1988*	890	1,600	-710

*preliminary.

SOURCE: Abreu et al. 1989:27.

1981 required over DR$9,000 to create one industrial job. It became obvious, then, that through the politics of IS the Dominican Republic was not going to fix the balance of payments, reduce the level of imports, or increase the level of production and sale. Even more importantly, the already alarming unemployment rate continued to grow.

Presumably, the adoption of the second strategy, the export-led economy, intended to increase the level of exports, remedy the balance of payment deficit, create new jobs, and reduce the level of unemployment. In sum, the new model sought to clean up the economic mess left by the IS model. But, as critics have argued, the problems have remained. The export-led economy has generated activities that function as economic enclaves, that rely heavily on foreign inputs and on hiring a labor force that possesses specific human capital qualities, and that depend on paying wages below the level required to have a decent living. Thus, in the end, both economic strategies have failed to establish a solvent economy for most of the Dominican people.

Thus, for the great majority of those who were looking for jobs, Dominican society was unable to satisfy their employment needs. It is true, as some have correctly claimed, that increasingly the economy was characterized by low wages, and that many employed workers were unable to fulfill their aspirations of social mobility. But a larger problem has been the growing lack of jobs for those who needed to earn a living.

If numbers serve to account for people's daily life stories, numbers then reflect that many more women and men are looking for jobs than the number of jobs available in that country. Many people are not looking for a better job, as some scholars on migration studies have argued; they are just looking for a job. The Instituto de Población y Desarrollo calculated that, from 1980 to 1990, the labor force was going to increase by approximately 90,000 new workers per year, but that the economy was going to produce only some 30,000 new jobs per year, leading to a wide disparity between job-seekers and jobs available in the labor market. But of course, these calculations were based on the fact that the birth rate would continue exactly as it was in 1980 (no women could afford to have an extra child); that the death rate would also remain constant; that the same number of people who leave the country for good would continue to do so; and that no Dominican would dare return home poor.

It is important to note that while the development strategies failed in their intention of creating a solid economy, free, for instance, of collapsing elements such as budget deficits and higher unemployment and underemployment rates, the strategies in question did not prevent or affect the capitalist accumulation process in the country. Quite to the contrary, while the economy continued to exhibit these disturbing symptoms, and most people, particularly from the working sectors, suffered the rigors of a harsh economy, the capitalist sectors have benefitted. They have capitalized, precisely, on the implementation of such development strategies.

The development of an industrial infrastructure that depended heavily on the use of foreign inputs for production led to trade deficits and loss of revenue. But the same infrastructure also contributed to the expansion of private industrial capital in the country and to the growth of international capitalism outside the geographical boundaries of the Dominican Republic. Thus, while Dominicans heard that the economy was not performing well because prices for Dominican products were falling precipitously, or that oil prices were too high in the international market and that the economy was being drained, specific economic indicators, such as net gain, capital investment, sales, and personal savings, show that for some the Dominican economy was performing rather well.

Table 2.6 indicates that, between 1970 and 1977, after deducting the cost of production, the industrial sector reflected a net capital gain of more than 38 percent per year. Similarly, from 1961 to 1981, the number of industrial establishments tripled. The value of sales increased fifteen times, just as the amount of capital invested in the manufacturing sector quadrupleted, going from DR$307 million to DR$1,259 million. The amount of capital deposited by Dominicans in U.S. and European banks from 1966 to 1983 increased sixteen times, from DR$53.2 million to DR$895 million (Moya Pons 1992:344, 405). It is important to add that while accumulation was taking place internally, in a similar fashion, foreign capital was increased through the internationalization of the Dominican economy as reflected in an increasing demand of import-related goods for production and consumption, as well as in an increasing foreign debt.

A comparison of the growth of the GNP and jobs shows that increasing unemployment rates, for instance, are not related to a falling GNP, as some may argue, but rather to the incapacity of the forces of production to create enough jobs. From 1970 to 1981, the aggregated value of the agriculture-ranching sector increased from DR$345.2 million to DR$483.9 million, reflecting an increase of 40 percent. But the number of employed workers in the sector increased by only 20 percent, from 502,634 to 602,908. During the same period, industrial production increased its aggregated value from DR$ 315.6 million to DR$703.8 million, reflecting an extraordinary rise of 123 percent. Yet, the number of workers in the sector increased by only 30 percent, from 113,040 to 147,086 (author's calculations from Santana and Tatis 1985:30).

TABLE 2.6 **Net Profit of the Industrial Sector, 1970–1977 (*In millions of DR$*)**

Year	Sales $	Cost of Production	Net Profit	Rate of Profit[*] (in %)
1970	583.3	390.6	192.7	49.3
1971	677.3	438.1	239.2	54.6
1972	826.2	521.0	304.6	58.8
1973	1058.4	690.0	368.4	53.4
1974	1478.1	1032.0	445.5	43.6
1975	1890.1	1252.0	637.2	50.8
1976	1821.0	1310.0	510.7	38.9
1977	2029.5	1456.4	573.1	39.3

[*]Formula: Rate of Profit = 3/2.

SOURCE: Lozano 1985:232.

Thus, at the end of the 1980s, Dominicans had experienced two development strategies that did not solve the socioeconomic problems of most citizens. Furthermore, for many sectors of the working class, when economic improvement has occurred, it has not translated into the creation of better jobs or enough new jobs to satisfy the demand. For many of the Dominican people, the behavior of the Dominican economy seems irrelevant. No matter how well the economy performed, their economic conditions did not improve, and their fate remained uncertain. For instance, the 1968–1975 period is identified by almost every economist as the time when Dominican society experienced the highest economic growth in its history, but the period witnessed growing inequality, poverty, and social distress. For many people, neither the '60s nor the '70s or '80s brought significant improvement to their lives. On the contrary, as indicated in table 2.7, which denotes changes in the distribution of income during the economic boom, in Dominican society the poor, through an invisible process of transference, became the poorest, while other social classes largely benefitted.

From 1969 to 1973, the groups of the population with the lowest income significantly reduced their share in the total income. These groups experienced an extraordinary loss of income, declining from 2.9 percent in 1969 to 1.4 percent in 1973, reflecting a loss of almost a half of their income in four

TABLE 2.7 **Changes in the Distribution of Income in Santo Domingo, 1969–1973**

Group of Income % of the Total # of Families	% of the Total Income of the Working Sectors	
YEAR	1969	1973
20% (lowest)	2.9	1.4
50% (low-middle)	17.6	15.4
30% (middle)	27.6	30.2
20% (top)	54.8	54.4

SOURCE: Lozano 1985:160.

years. While the top groups of the population continued to hold their share, concentrating 54.8 percent of the total income in 1969 and 54.4 percent in 1973, the middle-income groups experienced a significant increase in their share, increasing from 27.6 percent in 1969 to 30.2 percent in 1973 (Lozano 1985:160). Lozano argues that during Balaguer's first three presidential terms, the pattern of capitalist accumulation was based on the development of an industrial, commercial, and financial bourgeoisie, the exploitation of industrial sugar workers and the peasantry, and the expansion and consolidation of an urban middle class. He divides the middle class into two subsectors according to income and occupations, claiming that the lower middle class consisted of an enlarged bureaucracy of workers that had low earnings but was quantitatively important, while the upper middle class consisted of highly paid workers connected to the commercial and finance sectors. It was this last group of highly paid workers who, in Lozano's view, constituted the major consumers and buyers of imported goods and provided the main source of accumulation for the import bourgeoisie (160–73).

Poverty has increased considerably during the past thirty years or so in the country. In a national survey conducted by the Central Bank between 1976 and 1977, it was found that 51.3 percent of households in the country had a deficit in their monthly budget. These households earned 20.9 percent of the total income but had a consumption of 26.0 percent. The same study showed that 90 percent of the population did not consume the recommended amount of nutrients, and that 23.3 percent of the people were below the poverty level (Del Rosario Mota and Madera Daniel 1984). By 1984, 40.8 percent of children under five years of age were malnourished, and the number of families below the poverty level had doubled, rising to 47 percent, and increasing again by 1989 to 56 percent (Santana and Rathe 1993:189). (See Table 2.8).

Economists Isidoro Santana and Magdalena Rathe measured the poverty level in the Dominican Republic in the 1980s by using a methodology whereby the working population was

TABLE 2.8 **Poverty in the Dominican Republic (***Millions of people and*
*% of total population***)**

	1984	%	1989	%
Indigent	1.4	22.7	2.5	35.2
Poor	1.5	24.0	1.5	20.8
Total Poor	2.9	46.6	4.0	56.0

SOURCE: Santana and Rathe 1993:189–93.

classified according to household income and expenses and
divided into two groups. The poor were those below the poverty
line, and the nonpoor were above the line. Households where
60 percent or more of the income was spent in food were considered below the poverty line.

Indigent households were those that, even after using all
their income in food, could not obtain an appropriate diet.
They calculated that in 1989 the median poor (mid income
below the poverty line) needed to increase their income by 22
percent just to reach the classification of nonpoor. They
thought it unlikely that the gap between the poor and the nonpoor could be eliminated in the near future. They reasoned
that "if the income of all the poor began a sustained increase of
3 percent per year, even the median poor would need eight
years to leave the category of 'poor,' but that those poor with an
income below the mid-income poor would remain poor" (Santana and Rathe 1993:89–91; author's translation).

The 1980s were a difficult time for many workers. One could
no longer speak of a landless peasantry, an industrial proletariat,
(whether adhered to the sugar industries or the urban free-trade
zones), or workers in the informal economy. During the '80s, or
"the lost decade," in the words of economist Bernardo Vega,
most workers who needed to work for a living were affected.
During this time, the transference process—for the benefit of
the middle class, in particular, and sustained by Balaguer's economic policies—came to an end. Middle-class sectors now felt
that they were not an exception to the rule. They lost jobs, and
their salaries lost purchasing power. Stable and well-paying jobs

were increasingly replaced by less desirable jobs. Between 1980 and 1983, for instance, the number of employed people in the modern private sector decreased from 36.8 percent to 32.8 percent, but the number of workers in the informal sector increased from 26.7 percent to 32.5 percent (see table 2.9). Similarly, during the same years, the government jobs' median earnings declined from DR$251 to DR$233 (see table 2.10). From a middle-range analysis, one would conclude that the asphyxiating economic situation was generated by a fall in the price of Dominican export products in the international market and by an increase in the level of imports. But a historical-structural analysis would lead one to conclude that, in the end, the crisis was the result of a structurally deformed economy, mostly oriented to an export market and incapable of producing enough food or jobs to satisfy the needs of most Dominican people.

By 1978 Balaguer's first twelve years of rule came to an end. The Partido Revolucionario Dominicano (PRD) would govern from 1978 to 1986, the year when Balaguer would come to power again. Antonio Guzmán, the first PRD president, followed

TABLE 2.9 **Sectorial Evolution of Employed Population (*Santo Domingo*, *1980–1983*)**

	1980	1983	Rate of Growth
Government[1]	24.6	22.2	2.5
Modern Private[2]	36.8	32.8	2.0
Informal[3]	26.7	32.5	14.8
Domestic[4]	11.4	11.6	7.3
Others[5]	0.5	0.9	—
Total	100.0	100.0	6.6

[1]Includes all persons employed in state institutions, including central government, independent, semi-independent, or state industries.

[2]Includes all persons employed in industries, business, or private institutions with five or more workers. It also includes people with a university education, even if they work in places with less than five workers.

[3]Includes those persons with education below the university level and who work in private institutions and businesses with five workers or less. It excludes the domestic service.

[4]Includes all persons who work in the domestic service.

[5]Includes all persons not included in the above categories.

  SOURCE: Ceara Hatton 1990a:146.

the Keynesian model of direct government intervention by increasing the level of investments to stimulate economic activity and generate jobs. In effect, the period from 1979 to 1982 was characterized by an expansion of the aggregate demand through state investments, an increase of real salaries, and an increase in agriculture-ranching production (Ceara Hatton and Croes Hernández 1993:14) But unemployment remained high. The new jobs created, particularly in the public sector and the agribusiness industries (see tables 2.11 and 2.12) were simply not enough to address the severe unemployment problem. Similarly, jobs created in the public sector were nonproductive, and the agribusiness industries proved to be activities that, in requiring advanced technology and techniques, reduced the number of workers in proportion to the amount of capital invested.

Foreign debt also increased. The government financed its programs, including the creation of nonproductive jobs, by borrowing from foreign banks. At the same time, the price of oil went up in the international market, as the prices of Dominican export products fell precipitously. Between 1981 and 1982, the price of sugar fell 45 percent, tobacco 66 percent, gold 27 percent, and bauxite 67 percent (Ceara Hatton and Croes Hernández 1993). By 1982 the country, unable to pay its foreign creditors, was placed under an austerity plan by the International Monetary Fund, which strongly restricted the level of imports and froze workers' wages. By 1984 open unemployment reached 24.2 percent, by 1985 27.2 percent, and by 1986 28.7 percent. Inflation, on the other hand, increased from 7.7 percent in 1983 to 38 percent in 1984 and 47 percent in 1985 (Ceara Hatton and

TABLE 2.10 **Sectorial Median Income (DR$ monthly)**

Year	1980	1983	Difference
Government	251	233	-7.0
Modern	308	300	-1.6
Informal	195	181	-4.0
Domestic	58	55	-5.2

SOURCE: Adapted from Ceara Hatton 1990a: 184.

TABLE 2.11 **Investments and Jobs in Agribusiness (In DR$)**

Year	1983	1984	1985
Total Investments	112,031,707	49,676,234	156,793,476
Total Jobs Created	2,508	2,365	2,990
Agricultural Jobs	1,885	1,453	1,555
Industrial Jobs	623	912	1,435

SOURCE: Adapted from Moya Pons 1992:387.

Croes Hernández 1993:17). For the Dominican people, the economy reflected a state of severe crisis. For capitalists, however, the economy reflected the exhaustion of an economic model based on the production of traditional products and the sectoral relocation of capital.

Public Spending

During Balaguer's administrations, public spending was heavily concentrated in the construction of huge public projects, such as water-supply lines, roads, highways, public housing, parks, and monuments. The idea was to modernize and beautify the country, particularly the city of Santo Domingo, which by 1977 contained 70 percent of construction in the country. The construction agenda of the government sought to create jobs directly and to stimulate the economy (Serrulle Ramia 1984). But Balaguer's construction politics did not address social needs. If some projects generated social investments, such as the creation of a sewage system and water-supply lines, this was simply because they accorded with the interest of the government. Similarly, the construction policy demanded a heavy concentration of public funds in detriment to other areas. In 1989, 63 percent of total public funds was invested in construction (Santana and Rathe 1993:147).

But the level of investment in the public sector has been traditionally low in the Dominican Republic, as compared to other countries in the region. Historically, public investment has remained significantly below 20 percent of the GNP. But during

TABLE 2.12 **Dominican Republic Public Sector Workers, 1950–1986**

Year	Total	Year	Total
1950	40,476	1969	93,281
1951	47,703	1970	98,899
1952	50,391	1971	100,230
1953	46,429	1972	97,413
1954	42,292	1973	100,184
1955	55,390	1974	111,899
1956	61,692	1975	116,946
1957	71,269	1976	119,423
1958	77,926	1977	122,341
1959	81,546	1978	123,018
1960	84,934	1979	144,090
1961	88,026	1980	170,216
1962	110,349	1981	195,411
1963	112,568	1982	211,595
1964	112,002	1983	227,247
1965	99,159	1984	210,133
1966	97,999	1985	220,574
1967	98,728	1986	219,690
1968	96,584		

SOURCE: Gómez1985:25.

the "lost decade," investment in the sector declined dramatically, from DR$12.9 million in 1980 to DR$7.8 million in 1991 (Ceara Hatton and Hernández Croes 1993:98). A brief look at health indicators would show that social conditions have progressively deteriorated in this country. In 1964, for instance, there were 2.7 hospital beds per 1,000 people, decreasing to 1.2 beds per 1,000 people in 1984. While in 1980 the infant mortality rate (per 1,000 born) had been 29.7, by 1985 it became 58.6. Similarly, in 1988, 51.7 percent of the population did not have drinkable water, and 59.7 percent was still without a covered sewerage system (92). In general, in 1981 health programs received in real value DR$77 million, but by 1991 the amount went down to DR$54 million (Santana and Rathe 1993:171).

Public investment in education has been approached through the same inadequate funding policy. In the 1980s, the

proportion of the aggregate value of the GNP invested in public education was reduced in per-capita and real terms. Public
spending in education declined from 2.2 percent of the GNP in
the period 1978–1982 to 1.9 percent during 1983 to 1986, and
to 1.5 percent during 1987–1990. During the same time, real
per-capita spending declined by 60 percent (78). It is important
to also note that, just as in the United States, in the Dominican
Republic most of the public spending in education is absorbed
by salaries, particularly those paid to administrators who are
part of the school bureaucracy. By 1990, 90 percent of the funding allocated to public education went to salaries.

A General Assessment of Migrants and Migration from the Dominican Republic

During the 1970s, arguably one out of every four Dominicans migrating to the United States was likely to be a blue-collar
worker, specifically, an operative, and three in every fifty had a
professional or technical career. During the same decade, less
than one out of every two Dominicans was likely to have an
occupation at the time of migrating to the United States.[6] During the 1980s, the pattern changed slightly, since many more
Dominicans, particularly males, reported having an occupation
before emigrating. Although blue-collar workers continued to
dominate the migratory flow by a very large margin, that
decade featured more professional and technical workers
migrating than during the 1970s. The data reflect that during
the 1980s, more than one out of every two Dominican males
was likely to have an occupation before migrating, while less
than one out of every two women was likely to have one. Similarly, two out of every twenty-five Dominican males were likely
to have a professional or technical skill, while approximately
nine out of every twenty-five were likely to be an operative. One
out of every 14 women admitted reported having a professional
or technical career, and one out of every eight women was likely
to be an operative worker.[7]

The increase in the number of professional and technical workers migrating from the Dominican Republic during the 1980s, as
compared to the 1970s, corresponded to the progressive deterioration of public services, the drastic fall of the value of the *peso,*
and the loss of stable and well-paying jobs in in the Dominican
Republic. The 1980s was the decade when the International
Monetary Fund intervened with its austerity plan. By 1991 the
purchasing power of the minimum wage reflected half of the
value it had in the 1970s. And salary readjustment in the large
companies of the modern sector brought these salaries down to
60 percent of their value in the 1970s. As discussed before, during the 1980s, many members of the middle-class sectors could
not escape the negative effects of economic changes occurring
in the country. This time, they too were heavily impacted. If during the 1970s, the middle class in particular benefitted from the
expatriation of surplus laborers and the direct transferring of
resources from the poor and less privileged sectors, the economic restructuring of the 1980s provoked the dislocation of a
more diverse group, directly affecting many members of the
middle-class sectors and pushing them to seek the same solution
constantly sought by the less privileged groups.

As we have seen, the exodus from the Dominican Republic
to the United States accelerated during the 1980s. The number
of Dominicans leaving home progressively increased. Among
those who are still leaving the Island to come to the United
States, the proportion of those who are unskilled members of
the working class represents the overwhelming majority. The
majority of those who come are dark-skinned, and women pre-
dominate over men. These are facts. It is also factual that
Dominicans came to a society that was undergoing a transformation process, which has left the economy without the kinds
of jobs most of these new immigrants were equipped to do. To
make matters worse, they came into a racially stratified society,
where blacks and other dark people were marginalized, and
where, since the very beginning, poor Dominicans were not
needed nor wanted as workers. While doing research in the
Dominican Republic, Nancie González noted that "the refusal

rate on non-immigrant visas is surprising and significant. The two consulates together turned down 16,115 applicants for this type of visa in 1966. . . . Persons traveling on non-immigrant visas who have no intention of returning to the Dominican Republic in the immediate future . . . are the persons whom the U.S consulate would like to refuse visas" (1970:160). Gonzalez believed that those who were unlikely to return home were in reality economic migrants, produced by rural-urban mobility. They were neither tourists nor business people. They simply wanted to go to the United States to look for jobs and stay there. She was convinced that these job-seeking Dominicans were the ones who were likely to be rejected by the American consulates.

Finally, at the time when Dominicans began to arrive in the United States, Puerto Ricans had already been living here for decades without achieving significant economic progress. A team of social scientists who studied Puerto Rican migrants during the 1960s described the scenario awaiting the newcomers as follows: "Many of the [Puerto Rican] migrants are women, in a society where women's economic lot is still often difficult; many are Negroes, in a society in which color counts heavily against them; and most of the migrants—both Negroes and whites, both women and men—are without much skill, in a society where skill is increasingly important to adequate livelihood; and all enter a society where the opportunities for advancement seem increasingly too narrow for the poor, the uneducated, and the 'foreign' " (Mills, Senior, and Goldsen 1967:38–39). The irony is that the lugubrious scenario associated with Puerto Ricans decades ago accords fittingly with the situation that Dominican immigrants encounter upon their arrival in the receiving society. For now, two things remain to be seen: first, whether the changes adopted in the United States to curtail immigration, particularly those concerning blue-collar and unskilled workers, will leave the Dominican power structure without an open door to the United States, where surplus labor can be diligently and quietly expelled; and second, whether expelled Dominicans already living in the United States can make it as a group living in an unfriendly society that did not invite them.

PART 2

Settling in the Land of Dreams

3.

THE PERCEPTION OF A MIGRATORY MOVEMENT

Since the early 1960s, the number of Dominicans arriving legally in the United States has increased steadily. Scholars associate this influx with the aspirations of Dominicans to improve their material conditions in the receiving society, particularly through employment opportunities. Among the early researchers, Nancie L. González highlighted the way immigrant peasant Dominicans are integrated into the labor market of the host country. She explained that once in New York, it was not difficult for Dominicans to find jobs as waiters, cooks, dishwashers, longshoremen, garment workers, busboys, and the like. Perceiving migration as response to a demand for laborers, she affirmed that "these are the kinds of jobs which for some time have fallen to minority groups in New York. Puerto Ricans have been employed in these capacities in recent years, and we see a future trend in which Dominicans replace the former as they improve their economic and social status, intermarry with other Americans and lose their ethnic identity, or return to Puerto Rico" (González 1970:161–62).

González also sustained that uprooted Dominican peasants had a better chance of improving their lives in a large metropolitan city like New York than in a small one, such as Santo

Domingo. She differentiated the options in the two urban settings by saying that "it may be that the structure of the very large metropolis permits . . . a kind of protective pluralism which the smaller city cannot. Individuals, depending upon their previous life circumstances, may then fit into one of several kinds of urban living patterns. Thus, the peasant in cities like New York may survive very well using the techniques and social structures with which he grew up back in the Dominican Republic" (1970:170). In her view, Dominican peasants were able to adapt to the new city because they were equipped with what she identifies as "techniques and social structures," qualities to which the new city was receptive through its plurality.

Like González, Glenn Hendricks (1974) also emphasized the relative facility with which Dominicans allegedly found jobs once in New York City. Hendricks noted that prior to their arrival in the city, many Dominicans already had jobs waiting for them. These jobs had been secured by friends or relatives already established in the receiving society; this network of migrants eased the process of integration for the newcomers. During the 1960s and '70s, it was so easy to find work that, as Hendricks explains, Dominicans who wanted to return home for some time could do so without the fear of losing their current jobs. To illustrate his point, the author tells us the story of two cousins, Fabio and Rodolfo, who came together to New York and soon found jobs as helpers in the kitchen of a Hungarian restaurant. After a year, the chef taught the two cousins to cook and made them his assistants. When Fabio and Rodolfo decided to go home to visit their relatives, the owners gave them the option of leaving and coming back as dishwashers or staying until the closing of the restaurant for vacation so they could keep their positions as cooks. Fabio stayed, but his cousin Rodolfo went home. As a result, two months later when he returned, Rodolfo had to settle for the less remunerative job as dishwasher (Hendricks 1974:145). In the same vein, the bulk of the literature on Dominican migration published after 1979 suggests that once in the receiving society, Dominican immigrants have no trouble finding work.

While González believed that the demand for low-skilled workers resulted from the upward social mobility of minority workers, most subsequent scholars have felt that the need for low-
skilled labor in the manufacturing sector, for instance,
resulted from retiring white workers, as well as from the
restructured economy of the city. One gathers from the literature that the availability of jobs has to do with structural conditions, and that the network system Dominicans rely on, as
Hendricks has reported, simply facilitates the recruitment of
workers from a given ethnicity.

Sherri Grasmuck and Patricia Pessar have voiced a perception that typifies the prevalent wisdom in post-1979 scholarship.
They state that "the exodus of whites has caused an ethnic
realignment in the city. . . . As the non-white population
replaced whites, the former began to specialize in distinct economic spaces. Immigrants realized gains in every New York City
industry, but they came to be heavily over represented in the
declining manufacturing sector. This was especially the case for
Hispanic immigrants. . . . Self-employment, especially in firms
that cater to immigrant clients, is also often an important part
of the immigrant settlement process in places where immigrants abound" (Grasmuck and Pessar 1991:166–68).

An examination of self-employment among Dominicans
residing in New York City was tackled, first, by Roger Waldinger
(1986) and later by Alejandro Portes and Luis E. Guarnizo
(1990). These authors believe that self-employment among
immigrants comes as a direct response to dead-end and low-paying jobs in the receiving society. Waldinger explains the
entrance of Dominicans into the manufacturing sector as the
result of the city's economic restructuring, the relocation of
capital, particularly in manufacturing, and the exodus of Italian
and Jewish owners from the garment business. Portes and
Guarnizo, on the other hand, explain the development of
Dominican entrepreneurship in New York City from the perspective of the enclave economy. The enclave economy, as
defined by Portes and Bach in an earlier study of Cuban and
Mexican immigration in the United States (1985), refers to a

conglomerate of firms of any size owned and managed by members of a differentiated cultural or national minority.

But besides the facility with which Dominicans presumably
find jobs in the receiving society, the literature implies that
employment, either in the secondary job market or in the ethnic enclave, allows these immigrants the opportunities for
social mobility. The implication concerning social mobility is
two-fold. First, some scholars undertake to assess the socioeconomic status of Dominicans in the immigrant environment in
contrast to their former condition in the native land. Thus,
compared to things back home, Dominican migrants appear to
have moved up socially in the receiving society.[1] Second, many
scholars place emphasis on the upward movement of immigrant households in the native land through the invaluable
remittances sent by their relatives in the receiving society or
through investments they make in the homeland.

In examining the role of international migration in raising
the standard of living in the migrant's household in the native
land, Eugenia George has noted that, although remittances
from males living abroad stress the social subordination of
women, they also help to improve the women's socioeconomic
position. The author explains that "women who headed
migrant households in Los Pinos were less likely to work for pay
than nonimmigrant women. The fact that they did not need to
perform remunerated work was a sign of status" (George
1990:244).

The works of Portes and Guarnizo (1990) and Grasmuck
and Pessar (1991) make reference to the socioeconomic conditions of Dominican migrants within the context of the host
country. As its title indicates, *Tropical Capitalists* proposes that the
upward social mobility of Dominicans in the receiving society
comes through the development of an ethnic entrepreneurial
sector. The business sector, conceived initially to satisfy the
needs of immigrants, soon becomes a source of employment
that compensates for the dead-end and the low-paying jobs in
the secondary labor market. In explaining the functions of the
enclave, Portes and Guarnizo conclude that "patterns of social

interaction within the immigrant community create opportunities that, if not available to every one or in equal measure, offer
to many a means of escaping the drudgery and stagnation of
jobs in the secondary sector" (Portes and Guarnizo 1990:113).
In addition, the authors contend that the accumulation of capital, business knowledge, and skills in the United States among
Dominican entrepreneurs has spread over to the Dominican
Republic, where a capitalist sector with strong ties to Dominican
enclave in the United States has developed.

Grasmuck and Pessar approached carefully the issue of
social mobility among Dominicans residing in New York City.
They privileged the interpretation of the migrants themselves
as they spoke about their social status. In examining the
responses of Dominican informants in New York City concerning their social class, the authors conclude that "the majority of
our ethnographic informants, undocumented and women
included—68 of 100 informants—declare themselves to be
middle-class" (Grasmuck and Pessar 1991:195). The authors,
appropriately mystified about such self-classification, the vast
majority of whom had dead-end, low-paying, blue-collar jobs,
explain their informants' odd answers by arguing that Dominican immigrants tended to measure and qualify their immediate
surroundings according to values and standards current in the
Dominican Republic.

The authors believe that their informants' behavior reflected
a dual state of mind caused by the immigrant experience. They
reason that "the fact that the majority of our informants identified themselves as middle-class and drew on Dominican-based
referents in arriving at this self-attribution is emblematic of the
fact that Dominicans do indeed remain between two islands. On
the one hand, they embrace U.S.-manufactured items of consumption, transmogrified into Dominican models of consumption and standing, to shield themselves from a more objective, or
at least U.S.-centered, measure of their class position in New
York" (196–97).

In spite of what Dominican women may perceive as their class
status, Grasmuck and Pessar's study suggests that migration and

employment have granted to most of their Dominican informants membership into the working class of the receiving society. The same study suggests, however, that for Dominicans residing in the native land, the effects of out-migration differ notably.

The authors contend that emigration abroad has enabled many middle-class Dominicans in the home land to realize their class position. In other words, "Dominican out-migration has become a strategy of income accumulation for middle-class or aspiring middle-class households that cannot solidify their class position within the confines of the Dominican national economy" (201). Moreover, "the very visible housing developments that are associated in the minds of most with New York money support the premise that returnees have established solid middle-class life-styles in the Dominican Republic. Indeed, interviews with several Dominican bankers confirmed the fact that the great bulk of home mortgages in the Dominican Republic since the early 1980s have been granted to return migrants" (86).

The majority of migrant households interviewed by Grasmuck and Pessar derived most, or all, of their income from U.S. sources, which clearly reveals a high state of economic dependence on the part of these households. The authors conjectured that the economic dependence of these households would not disappear in the near future (87). Despite the fragility of their middle-class status, the authors feel that, in the end, through migration to the United States, Dominicans on the island do achieve their aspirations of social class mobility: "If we look at migration from the perspective of the migrant's stated intention of social mobility, then we must conclude that the migrants and their household members in the Dominican Republic have by and large been successful" (95).

Middle-class Dominicans residing in migrant households sustain their class status by remaining attached to the United States. They draw on resources secured by members of the household who emigrate abroad and seek temporary employment. Middle-class Dominicans who endeavor to find temporary employment in the United States in order to maintain their lifestyle in the native country seem to enter a process of *circular migration,* a term applied by Bonilla and Campos (1981) to the constant movement of surplus laborers who, during time of economic downs and high unemployment levels, moved back-and-forth between Puerto Rico and the United States. But while the evaluation of "middle-class" Dominican migrants in the homeland may lead one to take them for "circular migrants," or surplus workers who are pressed to move from place to place, the study by Grasmuck and Pessar shows the status of U.S. Dominican immigrants as bona fide members of the working class in the receiving society.

Pessar, the most prolific Dominican migration scholar in the United States has already addressed the issue of standard of living among Dominican women residing in New York City. Hers is a pioneering attempt to grasp the reality of living conditions for Dominicans in the city. Her ethnographic survey of fifty-five Dominican households and sixteen garment working women in New York City classified the households as poor and middle class. The author found that "*pooled* household, rather than individual, income enables many of the Dominican garment workers to maintain what they perceive is a middle-class standard of living" (Pessar 1987:112). The middle-class households in question were likely to have a low level of dependency (i.e., children and senior citizens who do not earn a salary) and more than one wage earner. Poor households, in contrast, normally showed a high level of dependency and fewer wage earners. In addition, middle-class households were found to have better "diet, housing, furniture, and use of leisure time" than poor households.

Pessar's study reveals the coexistence of two different social classes among Dominicans residing in New York City. Some women viewed themselves as part of the middle class, while others thought of themselves as poor. The author's own view on class differences among her informants can only be inferred from the values she assigns to the physical surroundings and material conditions of the two types of households included in her sample. Otherwise, her study privileges the self-classification of the informants, who were asked to name their social class. Pessar rightly observes that the perception of themselves as middle-class negatively affected her informants' behavior in the workplace: "This identification and satisfaction with improvement in life-style dampen the collective sentiments and solidarity that are potentially nurtured and ignited in the workplace" (113).

Similarly, the fact that some of the interviewees classified themselves as poor after migration raises the puzzling question of exactly what benefits emigration has brought them. Undoubtedly, Pessar's study opens a Pandora's Box: Have poor Dominican women, for instance, remained in the host country for lack of incentives to return to the native home?; how do these poor women fare in comparison with other poor women in the United States?; were they doing better or worse than the other women who were officially classified as poor in New York City?

Women whose households depended on income pooling and who tended to classify themselves as part of the middle class probably would attest to a different class status if questioned beyond their ability to spend. One could also problematize their self-classification as middle-class by eliciting an articulation of their self-perception based not on their class background in their native country, but rather on their current position in the host country (112). Income pooling enhances the living conditions of those poor households where the strategy is practiced, but only a comparative approach can tell us how well it serves the Dominican households in New York City. Income pooling is a budgetary strategy commonly used by poor working people who earn low wages, suffer high unemployment levels, and cannot separately satisfy the basic consumption needs of a single family. In that sense, income pooling hides the decreasing value of labor and the overexploitation of workers.

Pessar's study seems to suggest that income pooling and the ability to measure their standard of living by reference to their native country gave Dominican women a class identity that would otherwise have been impossible for them to acquire through the benefits derived from a single wage earner and an evaluation of themselves according to the socioeconomic standards of the receiving country. Leaving aside individual judgment, a question worth asking is, how real was these women's perception of their class affiliation? Besides, the women in Pessar's study, by virtue of their occupations, earnings, and living conditions were far removed from the socioeconomic indicators one commonly associates with the middle class.

Hard Work, High Poverty: Life in the Metropolis

In 1990, 73.1 percent of the Dominican men and 49.1 percent of the women sixteen years of age or older were active in the labor force. However, their relatively high labor-force participation rates did not exempt them from being poor or from falling under the poverty line in New York City.[2] The poverty line, an official measure of poverty provided by the federal government, refers to a minimum level of subsistence below which life becomes threatened. The definition is based on the amount of cash income received by a family before taxes.[3] Contrary to household income, poverty rates take into account family size, thus reflecting a fuller picture of economic distress among a given group.

In 1980, 1990, and 1996, compared with the New York City average, non-Hispanic whites, non-Hispanic blacks, and Hispanics overall, Dominicans had the highest poverty rate in the city (see table 3.1). One should also note that while, from 1980 to 1990, the poverty rate decreased for the other ethnic groups compared here, it increased slightly for Dominicans, from 36.0 percent to 36.6 percent. Similarly, in all three census years, Dominicans experienced poverty rates that were more than four times higher than the rate for non-Hispanic whites, the ethnic group with the lowest poverty rate in the city. Between 1980 and 1990, the difference in poverty rates between Dominicans and Hispanics overall, the two poorest groups in the study, became further accentuated as the former slightly increased its poverty rate, while the latter managed to reduce it by almost 4 percent.

Further examination of poverty among different types of families in the major Hispanic groups in the city reveals that

Dominicans continue to show the most dismal figures. The comparison of Dominican married couples with Puerto Rican, Colombian, and Ecuadorian ones shows that while in 1990 Dominican couples experienced a poverty rate of 20.8 percent, the other couples exhibited rates of 14.5 percent, 9.4 percent, and 12.2 percent, respectively, as indicated in table 3.2.

Families headed by a single parent tend to have lower incomes than those headed by married couples, whose income may likely come from multiple earners. Table 3.2 also contains a breakdown of poverty rates for female-headed families, defined here as families with a female householder and no spouse present. This table shows that Dominican female-headed families were worse off than their Latino counterparts, with a 59 percent poverty rate, followed very closely by 58 percent among Puerto Rican female-headed families. Ecuadorians and Colombian female-headed families showed rates of 40 percent and 28 percent respectively.

The persistent high rate of poverty among Dominicans is a direct reflection of a number of socioeconomic variables such as:

1. low earnings
2. high incidence of single-headed families
3. employment instability due to structural economic transformation and the loss of blue-collar and unskilled jobs, particularly in the manufacturing sector

TABLE 3.1 **Poverty Rate in New York City, 1980, 1990, 1996**

| | Poverty Rate in % | | |
Population Groups	1980	1990	1996
Dominican population	36.0	36.6	45.7
New York City average	18.0	17.2	23.8
Non-Hispanic whites	8.7	8.2	11.2
Non-Hispanic blacks	28.3	22.9	33.1
Hispanic population overall	35.0	31.4	37.2

SOURCES: For 1980 and 1990, Hernández, Rivera-Batiz, and Agodini 1995; for 1996, Hernández, and Rivera-Batiz 1997.

4. spatial segregation in low-growth job areas, such as the inner city versus the suburbs

5. low educational attainment in a school knowledge–based society

6. declining labor-force participation rates among men and women

From 1980 to 1990, the average earnings of Dominican men and women increased slightly, but, as the changes in earnings reflect, this growth did not compare with that of the other ethnic groups in the study, nor did it match the rate of inflation (see table 3.4). Scholars suggest that the combination of declining wages and high rates of inflation during the 1970s and 1980s pushed many families into poverty.

Harrison and Bluestone, the leading experts on what has come to be known as "the deindustrialization" of America, have convincingly explained the decline in the real value of wages and its effect on working people. They see the decline connected to the proliferation of low-paying jobs, which directly substituted well-paying industrial jobs. By 1979, they argued, "with wages falling and the government actively seeking to slow down (and eventually to reduce) some income grants to poor people, the negative effect of a worsening distribution of family income had become dominant" (Harrison and Bluestone 1988:135). Consequently, the absolute number of people ranking at below the poverty level grew considerably, from nearly 23 million in 1973 to over 35 million in 1983.

TABLE 3.2 **Family Type and Poverty Rate, 1990 (In %)**

Population Groups	Married Couple	Poverty Rate	Female-Headed	Poverty Rate
Dominicans	38.1	20.8	40.2	58.5
Puerto Ricans	33.8	14.5	36.0	57.9
Colombians	46.9	9.4	20.3	27.5
Ecuadorians	53.8	12.2	12.9	39.6

SOURCE: United States Department of Commerce 1994, 1990 Public Use Microdata, Census Sample A.

The decline in the value of wages and its effect on the working poor was also noted by David Ellwood, Robert Greenstein, and Isaac Shapiro, who, in a letter to *The New York Times*, explained that the purchasing power of low-wages had fallen drastically during the past decade. They noted that by 1989, the real value of the minimum wage was equal to the value it had in 1956, dramatically curtailing the purchasing power of workers (Ellwood, Greenstein, and Shapiro 1989). Similarly, the now-classic study of the black underclass by William J. Wilson noted how, during the 1970s, increases in the price of oil by OPEC countries gave way to recessions and inflations, causing the real value of wages to fall during the following years. Consequently, low-wage, unskilled, and ill-educated African Americans were driven into deep poverty (Wilson 1987:44–45).

The comparisons between full-time workers of Dominican descent and other major Latino[4] groups in the city reveal that Dominicans continued to hold the lowest earnings. Table 3.3 contains the mean earnings of full-time employed workers of major Latino groups in 1990, and it shows that while Dominicans had annual mean earnings of $14,778, Puerto Ricans had $20,159, Colombians $17,151, and Ecuadorians $16,027. Table 3.4 shows that among full-time Latino male and female workers sixteen years of age or older, both Dominican men and women had the lowest earnings in 1990.

In the New York metropolitan area, the poverty rate rose to 14.8 percent in 1991, from 14.3 percent in 1990 and 12.1 percent in 1989. Similarly, household purchasing power in 1991 was lower than in 1979. While all families compared here may have been severely impacted by the negative effects of declining wages combined with high inflation rates, these effects were compounded among many Dominican families who showed the largest household compositions and the lowest incomes. In 1990 the average Dominican household contained 4.7 persons. Almost one out of every two of these households was headed by a single woman, and over 50 percent of them fell below the official level of poverty. Table 3.5 shows that while, from 1980 to 1990, the poverty rate decreased for all female-headed families of major Latino groups compared here, among Dominicans, it increased slightly from 56.4 percent to 58.5 percent.

Some may argue that the high incidence of poverty among Dominican families stems from the combination of two vari-

TABLE 3.3 **Mean Full-Time* Earnings of Major Latino Groups, 1990**
          (Persons 16 years of age or older)

Population Grups	Mean Earnings	% Employed Ful-time
Dominicans	$14,778	83.7
Puerto Ricans	$20,159	83.3
Colombians	$17,751	84.0
Ecuadorians	$16,027	86.0

*Full time is defined as working thirty-five hours or more per week.

SOURCE: United States Department of Commerce 1994, 1990 Public Use Microdata, Census Sample A.

TABLE 3.4 **Mean Earnings of Full-Time Workers of Major Latino Groups, 1990**
          (Males and females)

Population Groups	Males	% Employed Full-time	Females	% Employed Full-time
Dominicans	$16,277	83.7	$12,791	80.2
Puerto Ricans	$21,331	86.6	$18,493	77.3
Colombians	$18,901	89.7	$14,766	77.4
Ecuadorians	$16,768	89.0	$14,711	81.3

SOURCE: United States Department of Commerce 1994, 1990 Public Use Microdata, Census Sample A.

TABLE 3.5 **Changes in Poverty Rate Among Latino Female-Headed Families, 1979–1989**

Population Groups	Poverty Rate 1979	Poverty Rate 1989	Changes
Dominicans	56.4	58.5	2.1
Puerto Ricans	67.8	57.9	-9.9
Colombians	32.8	27.5	-5.3
Ecuadorians	43.9	39.6	-4.3

SOURCE: United States Department of Commerce 1994, 1990 Public Use Microdata, Census Sample A.

ables: female-headed households and high dependency ratio. But a look at earnings among Dominican women may suggest yet another possibility. As reflected in table 3.4, Dominican women with full-time employment have earnings so far below the poverty line that unless they manage to secure some kind of assistance beyond their earnings, they would be unlikely to satisfy the basic needs of their households. With the poverty line set at $15,600 for a family of four in 1990, the average Dominican woman, head of a family of four and employed in a full time job, faced an income deficit. She was short by $2,809 just to bring her family to the poverty line.

Poverty rates can rise even when family incomes increase. But the data indicate that in the case of Dominicans, increasing poverty corresponds to low salaries, or the inability of the household head's income to support a family of four. Truly, high dependency ratios would aggravate the state of poverty among families depending on a single low-wage earner. Besides, a family may easily fall into poverty if headed by a woman in a society where women's market value is lower relative to men's. Similarly, a household whose members depend on more than one wage earner is likely to experience higher levels of consumption than a household with one wage earner. But in examining the case of the Dominican family, poverty involves more than high dependency ratios or gender issues. Here one needs to consider the wage factor itself as a fundamental cause of poverty. A state of poverty translates into the family's inability to reproduce itself socially. It is, in other words, their extremely low wages that leads the families to poverty. Rather than stemming strictly from the fact that Dominican families have larger households headed by single women, poverty among them includes as a variable the fact that those heads of households earn wages that are insufficient to support even a conventional family of four.

The conceptual association of female-headed households with poverty may well correspond to the patriarchal belief that conceives males as the only truly reliable breadwinners. This conception sees a woman head of household as a deviation, an anomaly, that may lead to economic or social problems. Connected with a bourgeois, orthodox, and unrealistic notion of what a family is and how it ought to be organized, the patriarchal bias conceals the true plight of women workers in the economy, chiefly their low value as compared to men. At a time when traditional and conservatives definitions of the family are being challenged by diverse alternative family structures, it behooves all of us to look beyond patriarchal ideas that are unequipped to explain economic hardship among women.

The Head of the Household: A Woman's Story

I would like to look at the case of a Dominican household headed by a female worker residing in Washington Heights to illustrate how a working woman, though holding down two jobs and working six days a week, can fail to earn enough to provide for her family. The worker's name is Doña Juana, a woman who first came to the United States in 1985. Her two boys, ages twelve and fourteen, followed her in 1988. Her brother, who was already living in the United States and had become a U.S. citizen, facilitated Doña Juana's permanent residence in this country. Doña Juana is a strong thirty-four-year-old woman, who only completed eight years of school in the native land. When I interviewed her in 1997, Doña Juana was working full-time in a garment factory owned by three Dominican brothers, but this was the fifth full-time job she had had since 1985. For twelve years she had moved between garment factories and the domestic sector. Once she left a job in a garment factory owned by a Chinese to work in another garment factory owned by an Indian man who paid her fifty cents more per hour and gave her a half-hour lunchtime. Eventually, she was laid off permanently from this job due to production slow down. None of the factory jobs had labor unions. None provided her with paid vacations.

Every one of Doña Juana's jobs sent her to the unemployment line at least once. The time of forced unemployment was invariably seen by the employer as her vacation. She explains that employers normally asked workers to consider the temporary lay-offs during slow-down periods as their vacation. Doña Juana, without much formal education, is an intelligent woman. She knew that "the bosses" were deceiving her and that she deserved paid vacations. But she felt that there was nothing she could do to stop the abuse. She would have to risk being fired, losing her job permanently, or settle for the unemployment benefits during the factory's difficult time while hoping to be rehired afterward. Once an employer even told her that he would send her home for three to four weeks, but that she could not apply for unemployment benefits since she was not being officially laid off.

The two domestic service jobs Doña Juana has held were both in New Jersey and paid $200 for a six-day work week. She first worked with a Cuban family and later with a Dominican family. She obtained these jobs through a Dominican contact who worked in a travel agency not far from her place of residence in Washington Heights. She had to leave the first job because the lady of the house wanted her to work nonstop from 8 A.M. to 6 P.M.. She left the Dominican family after she found out by chance that the couple's oldest son, who was bed ridden, had contracted AIDS.

Besides her current full-time job at the factory, Doña Juana cleans houses on a part-time basis. She works at this additional job on Saturday or Sunday; the day varies depending on whether or not the factory requires her to work on Saturday. She cleans two apartments, one of which is owned by a friend through whom I met Doña Juana in 1995. Doña Juana does not have medical insurance. Whenever there has been a medical emergency in her household, she has gone to a public hospital that normally charged her a fee in keeping with her meager annual earnings. Doña Juana has never applied for medicaid or food stamps because she does not want to jeopardize the possibility of bringing her mother here.

Figure 4 shows how Doña Juana distributes the income her current jobs generate. As indicated in the graph, her income

does not provide for other basic expenses, such as medicine, furniture, clothing, personal accessories, toiletries, and school sta-
tionary that are necessary for the social reproduction of the
household. Nor does it provide for any kind of emergency,
required gynecological check-ups, dental exams, or long-dis-
tance calls to her mother back home. How she manages to make
ends meet, what kinds of strategies permit her to survive, or
whether it can be said that she actually does succeed in her
efforts, go beyond the scope of the present discussion. For now, I
just wish to show that a gap does exist between the earnings of an
average Dominican woman worker and the income level deemed
necessary for the minimal subsistence of a regular family.

One needs to keep in mind, however, that Doña Juana's
case may not accurately represent the state of poverty of many
Dominican families in all its severity. Since she had been living
in the same residence for the past seven years, her rent was
about fifty dollars below the market value for a comparable
apartment in Washington Heights at that time. In addition, her
annual income was above the annual income of the average
Dominican working woman. Doña Juana's higher income
allowed her to acquire certain basic household items that may
have been outside the reach of the average earnings of most
Dominicans. The fact that Doña Juana had a phone, for
instance, and that in 1990 as many as 20 percent of employed
Dominicans sixteen years of age or older declared not to have a
phone in their residence, would indicate that Doña Juana was
much better off than the average low-wage earning Dominican
family.

In November of 1998, David Blum, a reporter for *The New
York Times*, examined the case of Amelia Garcia, a thirty-three-
year-old Dominican woman and a single mother of two young
children, whose earnings from her full-time job as a home
health-care attendant were insufficient to cover the basic needs
of her and her children. Blum felt that Garcia's case was a "vivid
example of the trap of poverty, which extends beyond welfare
recipients into the ranks of millions of working Americans." In
effect, Garcia's gross annual income, $10,800 ($6.25 an hour),

placed her family well below the level of poverty ($13,600 for a family of three). Blum explains that "nine years ago, [Mrs. Garcia] arrived in New York from Santo Domingo with the dream of working to save enough money to return to a better life in the Dominican Republic. But she has yet to earn much more than a dollar above the Federal minimum wage." Unable to save enough money to fulfill her dream of one day returning home, Garcia then seeks to accomplish more realistic dreams—the fulfillment of her household's basic needs. She "[seeks] out government assistance and charity, particularly at the end of every month when there is little or no money left. She waits for half-price sales at the Gap to buy clothes for her children: toys come at Christmas, if at all" and benefits derived from food vouchers, provided for youngsters five-years of age and younger, medicaid, and day-care programs, help Mrs. Garcia to accomplish her goals (Blum 1998:1).

Tables 3.6 and 3.7 contain data for 1980 and 1990 on the number of workers per Dominican household correlated with the poverty level. As table 3.6 shows, between 1980 and 1990, the tendency among Dominican immigrants was to increase the number of workers per household. The proportion of homes with three and four workers increased, and homes with one and two workers decreased. An observation worth making concerning the correlation in table 3.7 is that in some cases the simple adding of an extra wage earner to a given household may not necessarily alleviate its state of poverty. Between 1980 and 1990, for instance, the proportion of Dominican households with two workers that still fell below the poverty level increased by more than four percentage points. The effects of the number of workers in the economy of a given household would vary depending on the household's dependency ratios, the total composition of the household, and the actual amount of cumulative income.

Further computation based on the cumulative income and the total number of members in Dominican households shows the following scenario. In 1990, the average Dominican household contained 4.7 members and its average income was $27,005. Similarly, the per-capita household income amounted to $6,336, that is $115 dollars below the amount required for a single person under 65 years of age to be right at the level of the poverty threshold.[5]

Some may argue that persistent high levels of poverty among Dominicans is largely attributable to recent immigrants coming from the Dominican Republic. Tables 3.8a, 3.8b, and 3.8c contain data on two types of Dominican immigrants: those who arrived during the 1970s and those who arrived during the 1980s. The first had been living in the United States between eleven and twenty years, while the second had been living in the country between one and ten years. Both were present in 1990. Contrary to what some may have expected, these tables show that the socioeconomic status of many Dominicans does not improve with time in the United States. The poverty rate of immigrant households that entered before the 1980s, for instance, is 4 percentage points higher than those immigrants who arrived after the 1980s.[6]

TABLE 3.6 **Number of Workers in Dominican Households, 1980–1990**

Number of Workers	1980	1990
0	9%	10%
1	26%	22%
2	30%	28%
3	23%	25%
4	12%	15%

SOURCE: Candelario, López, and Hernández 1996.

TABLE 3.7 **Number of Workers in Dominican Households, 1980–1990**
(*Percentage below poverty level*)

Number of Workers	1980	1990
0	9.5%	9.0%
1	54.0%	56.0%
2	25.7%	30.0%
3	7.9%	4.0%
4	2.9%	1.0%

SOURCE: Candelario, López, and Hernández 1996.

The Washington Heights Dominican Community: The Construction of an Image

In *Out Of the Barrio: Toward a New Politics of Hispanic Assimilation* Linda Chavez (1991) compares the Puerto Rican community of the South Bronx and the Dominican community of Washington Heights. The displacement of a variety of small businesses along some of the streets of Washington Heights, which the author presumes to be owned by Dominicans, strikes her as illustrative of the immigrants living in the neighborhood. Contrary to the South Bronx Puerto Rican neighborhood, "whose streets were filled with men and women whose bearing suggested they had no place to go [and where] men stood in groups in vacant lots; women with baby carriages and toddlers in tow strolled slowly, aimlessly down the street" (Chavez 1991:152), in Washington Heights, Chavez was highly impressed by the commercial areas found in the community and by the energy displayed by people as they moved.

In *Tropical Capitalists: U.S.-Bound Immigration and Small-Enterprise Development in the Dominican Republic* (1990), Alejandro Portes and Luis Guarnizo emphasized the commercial sector of Washington Heights and its linkages to a similar operation in the Dominican Republic. They perceive this community as an economic enclave. The authors confess that they first approached the study of Dominicans in Washington Heights expecting to find a "concentration of immigrants in ghetto-like surroundings, where ethnic entrepreneurial activity is confined to a few grocery stores and restaurants plus gambling and pervasive street drug selling." But they were "genuinely surprised to encounter instead a thriving entrepreneurial community" (Portes and Guarnizo 1990:11).

The study describes Dominicans in New York who have opened up a variety of businesses that generate jobs for new arrivals. It is believed that the business sector represents an alternative for recent Dominican immigrants, who seek better job opportunities than those offered in the secondary labor market of the receiving society. Arguably, in these jobs Dominican workers learn, first hand, skills that are useful in commerce.

Portes and Guarnizo focused on Dominicans, who, having

TABLE 3.8a **Households Below Poverty Level (*Immigration from 1970 to 1979, and from 1980 to 1989, and present in 1990*)**

Status	1970s	1980s
Below Poverty Level	43%	39%
Total # of Households	28,560	30,719

SOURCE: Candelario, López, and Hernández 1996.

TABLE 3.8b **Households Below Poverty Level (*Immigration from 1970 to 1979, and from 1980 to 1989, and present in 1990*)**

Status	1970s	1980s
Below Poverty Level	43%	39%
100–200% Below	25%	31%
201–300% Below	17%	16%
400% Below	15%	14%
Total # of Households	28,560	30,719

SOURCE: Candelario, López, and Hernández 1996.

TABLE 3.8c **Households Receiving Public Assistance (*Immigration from 1970 to 1979, and from 1980 to 1989, and present in 1990*)**

Amount	1970s	1980s
Below Poverty Level	43%	39%
None	68%	79%
Up to $4,999	14%	11%
5K to $9,999	16%	10%
More than 10K	2%	0.5%
Total # Receiving Public Assistance	32%	28%

SOURCE: Candelario, López, and Hernández 1996.

returned home, owned businesses in the Dominican Republic at the time of the survey. The scholars established that as many as 84 percent of the returning capitalists had developed their commercial skills while employed in shops owned and operated by immigrants in the United States (19–20). Portes and Guarnizo describe the social relations among Dominicans in Washington

Heights that in their estimation form the basis for the formation and success of the Dominican entrepreneurial sector. They highlight primarily the solidarity and trust among members of the immigrant community. The resulting outcome—that is, the thriving and expanding entrepreneurial sector—falls within the community's funds of social capital.[7] The formation of social capital among Dominican immigrants and its impact both in the host society and in the native country through return migration strike the authors as a positive outcome resulting from the Dominican international migration process.

The above descriptions of Dominicans in Washington Heights allows little room for the kinds of stress one normally associates with the plight of a minority community in a society where groups with similar racial traits are known to experience antipathy and exclusion. That presentation, for instance, fails to imagine the groups of idle Dominican males who stand for endless hours on many corners along Broadway and other northern Manhattan avenues, and who annoy other Dominicans who try to avoid rubbing elbows with them on their way to and from work or as they walk their children to and from school.

Similarly, the ethnic enclave is construed as a safe haven where Dominicans can liberate themselves from the pressures of mainstream society. The community is portrayed as an autonomous entity, disengaged from the dynamics governing the rest of the host country. The Washington Heights described in the enclave model seems to relieve Dominicans of the social and legal requirements that burden other communities, such as immigration papers, income-tax transactions, and English proficiency.

However, workers may not find jobs nor better pay in the enclave economy. Gilbertson (1995) shows that Dominican and Colombian women in the enclave in New York City are exposed to higher levels of exploitation than women in the open economy. A study of Cuban and Chinese in the enclave showed that while the owners earned returns comparable to those earned by immigrant-minority entrepreneurs in the open economy, immigrant-minority workers of the enclave, however, received lower returns to human capital than immigrant-minority workers in the open economy. In a similar manner, the successful

Dominican film *Nueba Yol,* which dramatizes the travails of newly arrived immigrants, enacts the difficulty faced by a Dominican worker to find any job in the enclave and the pain of being exploited by a compatriot.

A Dominican man who migrated to New York City, Balbuena could not find a job for months. In Washington Heights he got menial, temporary, and jobs that paid badly, ranging from lifting heavy boxes in a grocery store to carrying large pieces of furniture in a store. The film's Washington Heights scenes depict Balbuena's unfruitful search for employment, as well as his sadness and despair at the sight of the moral breakdown of Dominican immigrants, as evidenced by the falling apart of the family and the involvement of many Dominicans in drug dealing. One memorable scene captures Balbuena's face with an expression of angry powerlessness after a long day's work resulted in being paid by his temporary Dominican employer an abusive amount. Obviously distressed, Balbuena protests, but in the end, without the protection that legal immigration papers may have afforded him, there is nothing he can do.

Balbuena came to live at a cousin's apartment where he becomes acquainted with the daily struggles of the average Dominican immigrant family. Made up by a working couple with three children, Balbuena's cousin and his wife held somewhat stable jobs. But they live modestly in an overcrowded apartment, dreaming about a better future for them and their children. The film enacts the other side of the Dominican story in New York, the real city opposed to the one imagined by prospective migrants back home. The closing scene shows Balbuena back in Santo Domingo, kneeling before the grave of his wife, as he explains to her the difference between the imaginary "Nueba Yol" that he had envisioned before migration and the real "New York" that he bitterly experienced as an undocumented alien. "Nueba Yol" is the land of milk and honey that exists in the minds of the uninformed populace. It is a city of gold, characterized by images of Hollywood and the magic land of Disney World. One can get rich easily there. Good and easy jobs abound. This modern city can help immigrants fulfill their dreams and secure a better future for their children. But, the latter, New York, is "otra cosa" (something else), Balbuena says. He speaks of the crude reality awaiting Dominicans when they get here: scarcity, unemployment, bad jobs, exclusion from productive areas, the alienation of not belonging, and the difficulty of even hoping to get what they came looking for.

The Untold Story: The Other Face of a Community

Census data indicate that in 1990, almost one out of every two persons in Washington Heights/Inwood was of Dominican descent, and that from 1980 to 1990, 78 percent of all new immigrants who settled in the neighborhood came from the Dominican Republic. Yet the census can only partially account for the actual number of Dominicans residing in Washington Heights, given the unknown portion of that community that has immigrated through informal channels. Washington Heights/Inwood is located at the north tip of Manhattan, extending from West 155th Street to West 220th Street. Alluding to the overwhelming presence of Dominicans there, the neighborhood now occasionally evokes such appellatives as "Quisqueya Heights" and "platano city."[8]

Young Dominicans growing up in Washington Heights may find it odd that, early in the twentieth century, historian Reginald Pelham Bolton ascribed to this area the most beautiful topography of New York City. Impressed by the Harlem and Hudson rivers, its many hills, and its scenic view of New Jersey, Bolton believed that Washington Heights residents were blessed (Bolton 1924). Unlike Bolton, many Dominicans do not experience Washington Heights as an idyllic terrain. The rivers, the hills, and the view of New Jersey still remain, but the natural beauty in the backdrop is outweighed by the ugly symbols of poverty, overcrowding, social destitution, and architectural decay.

In 1990 almost one in two Washington Heights Dominican households lived below the poverty line, and one in five did not have a phone. Table 3.9 shows the per-capita income, the poverty rate, and the lack of phone among the largest ethnic groups in Washington Heights for 1990. It shows that, by far, Dominicans have the highest percentage of homes without a phone, the low-est per-capita income, and the highest poverty rate among the groups compared. Tables 3.9 through 3.11 contain aggregated vital statistical data concerning poverty rates, health issues, schooling, and violence in the community of Washington Heights/Inwood. In every table, the comparison of 1980 and 1990 shows clear signs of increased levels of deterioration, mar-ginalization, and concentration of poverty. In 1990 Washington Heights/Inwood ranked third, after Central and East Harlem, among the five poorest communities in the borough of Manhat-tan. From 1980 to 1990 the number of people receiving public assistance increased considerably, jumping from 23 percent to 32 percent, and the number of families living below the poverty line increased from 24 percent to 28 percent.

Besides the high levels of unemployment, which through-out the 1980s had remained consistently higher in Washington Heights than in the rest of Manhattan and the entire City of New York, in 1990 this neighborhood also registered the high-est concentration of Medicaid births in the region. In 1990 four out of every ten children born in Manhattan and three out of every ten born in the City were insured by Medicaid. In con-trast, as many as seven out of every ten children born in Wash-ington Heights/Inwood were born under Medicaid, their mothers lacking any sort of private medical insurance.

The increased influx of Dominicans combined with dimin-ished construction and renovation of housing and school build-

TABLE 3.9 **Per-Capita Income, Poverty Rate, and Lack of Phone in Washington Heights/Inwood, 1990**

Population Groups	Per-Capita Income	Poverty Rate	Lack of Phone
Dominicans	$6,641	40.5%	20.0%
Puerto Ricans	$11,281	31.5%	10.9%
Other Hispanics	$11,174	29.4%	8.4%
Non-Hispanic whites	$21,331	15.3%	2.5%
Non-Hispanic blacks	$14,548	28.6%	9.8%
WH/Inwood Overall	$13,022	28.0%	

SOURCE: Garfield and Abramson 1995:15, 16, and 21.

ings led to overcrowding in Washington Heights during the
1980s. Population in the area reflected a 10 percent growth,
while housing units decreased by 1 percent. In 1990 the median
gross rent-to-income ratio in Washington Heights/Inwood was
31 percent. The neighborhood was among the top three with
the highest rent-income ratio in the borough of Manhattan. The
high rents and the rising demand for housing forced many families to double-up within single housing units. Table 3.10 shows
that, from 1980 to 1990, the number of families increased by 181
families, the number of householders went down slightly by 914
people, and, consequently, the percentages of crowded and
overcrowded households doubled.

TABLE 3.10 **Selected Demographic Indicators in Washington Heights/
Inwood, 1980–1990**

Indicators	1980	1990	Change in %
Population	179,941	198,192	10.1
% Pop. receiving			
public assistance[+]	23.1	32.4	55.0
	(41,485)	(64,208)	
# of households	70,655	69,741	-1.3
% of crowded[*]			
households	11.0%	22.0%	50.0
% of overcrowded[**]			
households	4.0%	10.0%	40.0
# of families	44,978	45,159	0.4
% below poverty level	23.9	27.5	15.3
	(10,759)	(12,397)	
# of families with			
female head			
of household	14,624	18,323	25.3
% below poverty level	63.9	70.1	26.4
	(6,879)	(8,6⬛)	
Total housing units	73,566	72,553	-1.38

[+] Includes AFDC, Home Relief, Medicaid, and Supplemental Security Income.
[*] Crowded Households contain more than 1 person per room.
[**] Very crowded households contain more than 1.5 persons per room.
   SOURCES: New York City Department of City Planning: *Socioeconomic Profiles: A Portrait of New York City's Community Districts from the 1980 and 1990 Censuses of Population and Housing*, 1993; *Community District Needs: Fiscal Year 1993*, Manhattan.

The increased demand for housing led to speculation among some landlords and superintendents, who sought to exploit the situation through informal arrangements whereby even the basements of their buildings exacted high rents. As a result, today any apartment building located in certain areas of Washington Heights/Inwood may contain more apartments than the number dictated by the architectural plan when the building was constructed. The spontaneous, informal living arrangements normally take the form of individual rooms of different sizes that are rented by single tenants or a whole family. The often improvised rooms, built around garbage depositories and incinerators, often violate safety and sanitary housing regulations.[9]

At the time Dominicans arrived in the city, the labor market had began to require workers with school-generated skills (see chapter 3). For workers, going back to school (trade school, college) for training, retraining, or updating their knowledge became an important trend. Thirty years later the trend continues. Today the more formal education one has, the higher one's earnings are likely to be. When we look at Dominicans in the school system, serious doubts inevitably arise concerning their prospects for producing a competitive generation of highly trained workers.

A 1994 study on school enrollment growth in the public system found that within the borough of Manhattan, only School District 6, the district with the largest number of Dominican students, was included in the list of the ten most overcrowded school districts in the New York City region. Out of the twelve elementary and intermediate schools in District 6, three suffered from extreme overcrowding. The year before, District 6 had figured among the school districts in the city with the lowest percentage of pupils scoring at or above grade level either in reading or mathematics. Washington Heights Community Planning Board 12 argued that is was very difficult for children to learn in overcrowded classrooms located in old buildings that were falling apart and leaking noxious gasses (*Community District Needs* 1991).

Besides the alarming math and reading scores, overcrowd-ing, and dilapidated buildings at the elementary level, Domini-can students also encounter serious difficulties in high school and college, which impact their educational outcomes. In a recent ethnographic study conducted at two high schools in Manhattan that are largely populated by Dominican students, Nancy López found that institutional factors, such as the dis-parity in funding among public schools, influenced dropout and graduation rates among the students.

Studying schools that registered the highest dropout and lowest graduation rates in the city, López also looked at those students who applied for admission to the City University of New York. She found that only 2 percent from one school and 13 percent from the other were able to pass the freshman entrance examination (López 1996). Other institutional data support López's findings. The U.S. census data shows that the proportion of U.S.-born Dominicans in college dropped from 16.7 percent in 1980 to 12.2 percent in 1990 (Hernández, Rivera-Batiz, and Agodini 1995).

Washington Heights is a neighborhood where parents fear

TABLE 3.11 **Selected Health Indicators in Washington Heights\Inwood, 1980–1990**

Indicators	1980	1990	Change in Absolute #
Total # of Hospitals	9*	1	-8
Years of Productive Life Lost due to**			
Homicide		2,778	
AIDS		1,569	
Malignant tumors		1,234	
Heart disease		1,061	
Cerebro-vascular disease		200	
Tuberculosis infection rate***	26.5	71.6	45.1

*Hospitals in or near the area.
**Calculation of years of productive life lost combines data on the death rate with the age of those who die.
***Rate for 100,000 population.
SOURCE: Garfield and Abramson 1995:34–37.

TABLE 3.12 **Selected Indicators of Violent Crimes in Washington
            Heights/Inwood, 1980–1990**

Indicators*	1980	1990	Change in %
Murders	20	52	61.5
Rapes	41	33	-19.5
Assaults	215	570	62.2
Robberies	944	968	2.5

*Rates per 100,000 population.
   SOURCE: Garfield and Abramson 1995:22–23.

that their children, on the way to school, the parks, or play-
grounds, might be caught by stray bullets from drugs-related
shoot-outs. Tables 3.11 and 2.12 show the levels of violence and
health risks in the community. As indicated in table 3.11, in
1990 a person in this community was more likely to die violently
than by AIDS or any other of the common diseases that figure
at the top of the most frequent causes of death in the United
States. Table 3.12 indicates that during the 1980–1990 period,
instances of rape declined considerably in the area, but murder,
assault, and robbery all increased significantly.

Marginalization and Poverty Among Dominicans: An Assessment

The data presented in tables 3.1 through 3.12 lead one to
conclude that most Dominicans confront economic hardship
and poverty in the receiving society. Poverty among Dominicans
could be partially explained from the perspective of the disparity between the skills Dominicans possess and the exigencies of
an specialized labor market, as shown in chapter 3. Many
Dominicans have no jobs while others are poorly paid. Their
employment experiences clearly reflect that they did not come
to occupy booming job markets or to occupy jobs that awaited
them. While most Dominicans have moved in search of economic progress and a better life, for now the receiving society
has failed to satisfy their specific needs and aspirations.

The difficulty of employment and, in general, the hard times encountered by most Dominicans in the labor market would seem to challenge the theoretical understanding that perceives the mobility of workers as a direct response to the labor-market needs of the host country. The case of Dominican immigrants raises these simple questions: If their labor was so badly needed in the United States, why has their relationship with the labor market been so erratic? And why have unemployment rates remained so high among Dominicans, as chapter 3 shows?

The current conditions of most Dominican migrants add new insights into the understanding of the mobility of people to advanced societies. It seems probable, for instance, that for many, moving from a developing society to an advanced one in search of economic progress and better opportunities may not necessarily lead to a materialization of their aspirations. Indeed, the foregoing discussion suggests the possibility of a disparity between the needs, aspirations, and motivations of the migrants who move and the needs, possibilities, and willingness of the host country to receive them.

Today one could safely say that poverty and marginalization among Dominican migrants result from their migration and settlement into a society that has been unable to absorb them effectively into the process of production. As a result, a large number of Dominicans have, for the most part, joined the ranks of the working poor, a historically forgotten segment of the American population, whose diversity, increasing number, and persistent poverty in spite of economic booms have inspired an abundant amount of writings. These Dominicans, although their future is as uncertain as that of most poor, are really lucky. An equally impressive number of Dominicans have been less fortunate in the immigrant land. Their poverty increases beyond that of the working poor; their unemployment rates continue to increase, because they have not been able to find jobs since their factory moved out of Manhattan to another state or country; they have dropped out from the labor force and have affected the participation rates for all adult working

Dominicans. These are the ones who are joining the ranks of the absolute surplus population. As a society, the question we still need to address, however, is whether Dominicans' present socioeconomic condition represents a typical and temporary stage, identified with any new immigrant group in the process of integration, or whether we are witnessing a situation that, if not effectively and timely addressed, is likely to become permanent for the majority of Dominican people in the immigrant land.

4.

DOMINICANS IN THE LABOR MARKET

The experience of immigrants in the labor market of the receiving society is commonly used as a reliable measure of their economic progress. Their place in the job market, earnings, rates of labor force participation, and patterns of employment and unemployment are among the salient variables that indicate the status of immigrants in the labor market. At the same time, each one of these variables is affected by the type of workers the productive market needs and the value ascribed to the immigrant workers' abilities and skills. If the abilities and skills of an immigrant group are badly needed and highly valued in the receiving society, that group will most likely have high rates of employment and competitive earnings. The labor market experience of the same immigrant group, however, would be quite different if its abilities and skills are found in abundance and therefore depreciated in the receiving society. In the end, the material well-being of immigrants would be determined not only by their incorporation into the labor market of the receiving society but also by the nature and effectiveness of that incorporation.

Dominicans as Workers in New York City

Dominicans are economic migrants who have moved out of the Dominican Republic in search of a better life. Their migratory flow, which began after 1966, has continued to increase, accelerating particularly during the 1980s. According to the U.S. census, in 1990 there were 511,297 Dominicans living in the United States, and more than 65 percent of them were residing in the state of New York.

In 1990 New York City in particular accounted for mre than 93 percent of those Dominicans who were living in the New York State area. As indicated in table 4.1, from 1980 to 1990, the Dominican population of the city increased from 125,380 to 332,713 to become the ethnic group with the largest growth for that period. As indicated in figure 1, their remarkable numerical gain was the result of a constant and growing immigration influx, combined with high fertility rates among Dominican women, particularly in New York City.[1] The massive number of arriving Dominicans occurred at a time when New York City was undergoing socioeconomic restructuring in the labor market. This transformation would have a remarkable impact on the need for and value of labor, as well as the creation of jobs.

The socioeconomic restructuring of New York City, which has been well studied and documented by other scholars, is beyond the scope of this book. The present study will only look

TABLE 4.1 **The Dominican Population of New York City, by Borough**

New York City Borough	1980	1990	% of Total Dom. Pop., 1990
Manhattan	62,660	136,696	41.1
The Bronx	17,640	87,261	26.2
Brooklyn	21,140	55,301	16.6
Queens	23,780	52,309	15.7
Staten Island	160	1,146	0.4
Total	125,380	332,713	100.0

SOURCE: Hernández, Rivera-Batiz, and Agodini 1995.

briefly at those details that may help to explain the position of Dominicans in the labor market of the city.

The restructuring of the city has involved a transformation from an economy based predominantly on industrial production to one based on services. As a result of this change, today New York City is commonly classified as a postindustrial city. Scholars generally agree that some time during the 1950s, the large manufacturing sector that had characterized the economic life of the city began to shrink. The shrinking process manifested itself in the disappearance of hundreds of thousands of manufacturing jobs, particularly in the garment industry, the largest area of industrial production. From 1969 to 1985, for instance, the city lost 465,000 manufacturing jobs (Drennan 1991:29). The restructuring process dislocated productive jobs, as well as a whole variety of other jobs that were tangentially connected to the manufacturing sector. Entire industrial headquarters moved out, and with them went employment opportunities. From 1969 to 1989, for instance, employment in wholesale trade declined from 309,000 to 229,000, and in trucking and warehousing the number went from 41,000 to 26,000 (Drennan 1991:32). But, overall, the decline in employment occurred primarily among blue-collar and unskilled workers, who suffered from 1970 to 1986 the loss of 510,000 jobs in fields that required less than twelve years of education (Kasarda 1990).

The Larger Economic Picture

The dislocation of jobs came not only as a direct result of the shift of the economy from manufacturing to service but also from downward economic trends affecting the nation. Robert Pollin has pointed out that at the national level, "stagnation of the U.S. economy since the mid-1960s has been apparent in high unemployment rates and declining real wages, in slower overall GNP growth and low-capacity utilization, and the downward trend of capital profitability" (Pollin 1989:123). These economic problems, Pollin argues, were exacerbated during the 1970s, when, in an attempt to reverse the negative effects by inducing growth, the country adopted the strategy of increasing the public debt. While borrowing enabled the corporate sector to invest without affecting its already reduced levels of profits, the government relied on borrowed funds to continue its expenditure and fuel its policies for growth.

The national trend had profound repercussions at the regional level. Andrés Torres and Frank Bonilla show that since the early 1970s, the New York region has experienced a downward economic movement, as may be gathered from employment growth, production output, and personal income. The authors explain that "between 1972 and 1982, for example, the Gross Regional Product fell as a proportion of Gross National Product from 12.3 percent to 10.9 percent. . . . There was a parallel erosion of shares in total employment (from 9.7% to 8.6%) and aggregate personal income (from 12.5% to 10.0%)" (Torres and Bonilla 1993:88).

As indicated in figure 4, general unemployment remained high in New York City, often exceeding the national average. Unemployment began to decline in the mid-1980s only to rise again, reaching in 1992 the high levels of the 1970s. Although by 1982 the city had entered a stage of brief economic recovery, it was really due to "falling labor participation rates and declining employment population ratios" that unemployment rates showed perceptible reductions (Torres and Bonilla 1993:88).

To have a clear grasp of the effects of job dislocation, particularly on workers in blue-collar and unskilled jobs, one need only look at the profile of groups normally associated with the labor market in question. In that respect, Clara Rodríguez has cited among the major factors causing a high incidence of poverty and unemployment in the Puerto Rican community during the 1950s and 1970s in New York City the narrowing of the manufacturing sector that had been the group's major source of employment at the time of its arrival and still concentrated 60 percent of its labor force by the 1960s (Rodríguez 1979:208). Scholars have found similar effects among African

Americans. William Julius Wilson explains that the loss of manufacturing jobs, which had traditionally been a niche for black
workers, had a tremendously negative impact on the well-being
of that community, resulting in considerably high degrees of
social distress, poverty, and disempowerment. Wilson adds that
today the low educational attainment of blacks, as well as their
pattern of concentration in urban settings, hamper their ability
to gain employment in the rising service sector or in the new
blue-collar and unskilled jobs that are generated in suburban
areas (Wilson 1987:39–41).

The described scenario would suggest that this period of
economic transformation has been a tough time to be an
unskilled Puerto Rican or black worker. Indeed, these two
groups have endured trying times caused by poverty and job-
lessness, as well as budgetary deficits stemming from economic
downturns. For many residents, leaving the city became the
only feasible option. In the 1960s, whites began to leave the city,
and their flight would accelerate in the two decades that followed. By 1970 Puerto Ricans and blacks joined all those who
could afford to exit the city and packed up and left. The census
indicates that, from 1970 to 1980, New York City lost 10.4 percent of its overall population, a net total of 824,261 persons.

The Restructuring of the Economy: A Theory of Job Creation

In *The Mobility of Labor and Capital* (1988), Saskia Sassen
states that the shifting of the economy from manufacturing to
services generated a need for unskilled migrant workers. Sassen
contends that contrary to what many believe, cheap immigrant
labor is employed not only in decaying economic sectors but
also in growing productive areas. The shifting of the economy,
she adds, created global cities where the development of
advanced service sectors resulted in the creation of new blue-
collar, low-paying jobs and the expansion of the informal economy. Similarly, industrial production did not disappear.
Instead, it was transformed, generating in the process new low-

paying jobs. Thus, the demand for a low-value labor force was sustained. Sassen incorporates post-1965 immigrants into the labor force that would take on these new jobs.

Sassen explains the economic shift as one whereby large manufacturing industries based on standardized, capital-intensive production were replaced by the development of another type of industrial option represented by small industrial settings, scarce mechanization, and intensive use of labor. Due to the recurrence of sweatshops, low-wages, dead-end jobs, and lack of unionization, Sassen has referred to this industrial development as a "downgraded manufacturing sector" (23). She adds that the expansion of the service sector has involved not only the generation of highly paid professional and technical jobs but also a vast infrastructure of low-paying service jobs that require low levels of skill and minimal language proficiency. Using data from a survey from the New York State Department of Labor, she shows that "of all occupations in all the service industries covered by the sample, 16.7 percent were identified as low-wage jobs: of these 10.8 percent were in finance, insurance and real estate; 23.9 percent were in business services, and 18.9 percent were in the remaining service industries" (158). Jobs associated with this sector rely on poorly-trained workers since they include low managerial and clerical positions, as well as undesirable shifts at night or on weekends.

Besides, high-paying service-sector jobs have a way of generating low-paying jobs. Patterns of consumption of highly paid workers facilitate the creation of jobs associated with their lifestyles. Many of these jobs, Sassen adds, are part of the underground economy and include "the preparation of specialties and gourmet foods, the production of decorative items and luxury clothing and other personal goods, various kinds of services for cleaning, repair, [and] errand-running" (158). She states that the relative shortage of labor in certain locales in the host country is what largely explains the demand for immigrant workers and their move into specific cities.

Jobs became available at a time when the native supply of low-value and powerless workers decreased in so far as the formerly available pool consisted of workers who "have become politicized, are unwilling to take highly undesirable jobs even if they pay minimum wage, and have access to welfare as an alternative to low-wage jobs" (39–40). Moreover, unionization, among some, and "weak labor-market attachments," among others, have affected the availability of a native source of cheap labor (128). In addition to their function as workers in a society facing a relative shortage of labor, immigrant workers, Sassen adds, are attractive to employers for their low-wage status, as well as for their lack of negotiating power (40).

Sassen has brought forth a new argument and fresh analytical insight to sustain the belief that the arrival of immigrant workers coincides with a demand for low-wage workers. Yet increasing unemployment levels, particularly among minorities and unskilled workers, and systematic economic downturns provided the grounds for believing that the mobility of labor and capital (whether national or international) essentially meant a search for maximizing profit and the increasing displacement of workers. And while many had began to question the abilities of modern capitalist societies to create enough jobs and their need for an increasing pool of workers—whether native or immigrants—Sassen found sources of employment that created the demand for a variety of low-skilled immigrant workers. Thus, her work provided a direct answer to those who questioned, on the grounds of job shortages, the increasing entrance of new job seekers. The experience of Dominicans, however, would seem to defy the correlation between immigrant workers and labor demand in the United States. Dominicans, for the most part, have not come to occupy booming low-wage job markets. Nor can it be argued that the host society shows a need for Dominican workers. Using 1980, 1990, and 1997 data from U.S. censuses, the next section will describe and explain the position of Dominicans in the labor market of New York City after three decades of migration.[2] The idea is to show how a migratory movement of blue-collar job seekers can coincide perfectly with a period of job shortage in the same labor market in a receiving society.

Industrial Distribution of Dominican Labor Force

As indicated in table 4.2, industrial distribution during the 1980s and 1990s of the ethnic groups compared in this chapter[3] suggests that in both decades Dominicans had by far the highest percentage of people employed in manufacturing. In 1990 a total of 25.7 percent of Dominicans sixteen years of age or older worked in the manufacturing sector. During the same year, the percentages for Hispanics, including Puerto Ricans, was 18.6 percent, for non-Hispanic whites 10.9 percent, and 8.2 percent for non-Hispanic blacks. Compared to 1980, in 1990 Dominicans, as well as the other groups, considerably reduced their participation in the manufacturing industry. The reduction is connected to the overall shift that started in the 1950s and has led to a transformed economy. It may be said to have had a disproportionate impact on Dominican workers, who experienced a decline from 48.6 percent to 25.7 percent, that is, nearly half of those employed in the sector.

TABLE 4.2 **Industrial Distribution of the Labor Force, New York City, 1990**

Industry	Non-HW	Non-HB	Hispanic	Dominican
Agriculture, forestry, and mining	0.5	0.3	0.5	0.3
Construction	4.9	4.2	4.9	4.3
Manufacturing	10.9	8.2	18.6	25.7
Transportation and public utility	8.2	11.7	7.6	6.6
Trade	17.9	14.1	22.5	27.6
Finance, insurance, real estate	13.1	10.1	8.6	5.5
Professional services (health, education)	28.7	32.0	19.7	14.4
Business services	6.2	7.1	7.0	6.8
Personal/entertainment services	5.5	5.8	7.0	7.0
Public administration	4.1	6.5	3.6	1.9

SOURCE: Hernández, Rivera-Batiz, and Agodini 1995.

The drastic loss of manufacturing jobs among Dominicans is connected to a sectoral decline and the market's inability to reabsorb workers after its transformation. Since the 1950s, the manufacturing sector has experienced an increasing loss in jobs, and the industry's creation of new jobs has not sufficed to alter the decline. As Sassen correctly notes, the manufacturing industry began a process of change that eliminated many jobs and generated others. A reflection of that change is the proliferation of thousands of small firms established throughout New York City and the neighboring borough of Long Island, whose production is not standardized or oriented to a general public. These customer-oriented small firms cater to the needs of small clienteles. However, these new firms, ranging from electronics (particularly for the defense industry) to apparel and furniture, manage to employ only a small fraction of the total labor force of the city (O'Neill and Moss 1991:10).

The limited capacity of job creation exhibited by the new industries accords with the fact that many of them do not require a large workforce for production. Generally, these industries produce for a small and selective clientele, whose primary requirement is quality not quantity. Moreover, production in these industries is organized around what is called "intellectual capital," meaning the combination of "patents, processes, management skills, technologies, information about customer and suppliers, and old-fashioned experience" as defined by O'Neill and Moss (1991:9). That is to say that although these industries could draw from an intensive use of labor rather than of capital, their level of output is reduced in scale. Moreover, their production remains linked to an overall labor force, which ultimately cannot be completely unskilled.

Similarly, the creation of jobs in the manufacturing sector is linked to trends in the national economy. Thus, while jobs in the industries associated with the production of durable goods, including cars, computers, furniture, and appliances, experienced some increases as a direct result of national growth during times of economic recovery, jobs in the apparel industry, particularly those associated with fashion, have undergone a constant decline. In particular, the apparel industry, which is the largest area of production within manufacturing and the one that absorbs the largest number of Dominican workers, did not expand its number of jobs, although it did respond to local demand by transforming into small shops oriented to the production of elaborate and expensive clothing for exclusive customers. In fact, from 1984 to 1985, the apparel industry lost 12.5 percent of its share in the labor market without regenerating an equal number of jobs in the years to follow (*Annual Report on Social Indicators* 1991:44).

Table 4.2 also indicates that in the 1980s, Dominicans began to move to the service sector, as evinced by their increasing participation in trade and professional services. Compared to the other ethnic groups, Dominicans had the highest percentage of people employed in trade in 1990. While for Dominicans, employment in trade represented 27.6 percent, for non-Hispanic whites it represented 17.9 percent, for non-Hispanic blacks 10.1 percent, and for Hispanics 22.5 percent. Trade among Dominicans is associated with employment in retail trade, particularly in eating and drinking establishments, grocery stores, apparel shoes, and accessory stores.

The movement of Dominicans to the service sector has in no way compensated their loss of jobs in the manufacturing industry. To the contrary, their movement has been characterized by an absolute loss of jobs as reflected in an increase in unemployment and a decrease in labor force participation rates. If one closely follows their sectoral movement, one will see that a clear pattern begins to emerge, a pattern which reflects that Dominicans are caught in a no-win situation. They are faced with expulsion from a declining job market and inclusion into sectors of a job market that happens to be characterized by slow or negative growth.

In short, while Dominicans have increased their participation rate in the service sector, the participation itself is quantitatively limited and involves an association with the least dynamic job markets of the service sector. As figure 7 shows, substantial growth in the service sector has occurred within the

FIRE (finance, insurance, real estate) industries, as well as in
government jobs, and not in trade or TCPU (transportation,
communication, and public utilities), two of the three service
sector job markets where the participation of Dominicans has
moderately increased. Trade and TCPU in general were characterized by absolute job loss in the 1980s. Table 4.2 also indicates that compared to other ethnic groups, in 1990 Dominicans had the lowest representation in the FIRE industries as
well as in public administration jobs. In the FIRE industries, a
total of 5.5 percent of Dominicans gained employment in the
market, while the percentages for the other groups were 13.1
percent for non-Hispanic whites, 10.1 percent for non-Hispanic
blacks, and 8.6 percent for Hispanics.

Occupational Distribution

Occupational distribution among Dominicans clearly indicates that compared to the other ethnic groups, Dominicans
are highly underrepresented in the professional and managerial categories. As indicated in table 4.3, in 1990 a total of only
9.6 percent of Dominicans gained employment in professional
and managerial jobs, compared to non-Hispanic whites
(38.5%), non-Hispanic blacks (19.6%), and Hispanics (13.9%).
Dominicans also have the highest proportion of workers
employed in blue-collar and unskilled jobs (laborers, fabricators, and operators). While 30.9 percent of Dominicans worked
in blue-collar occupations, the percentages for the other
groups in that sector are 7.6 percent for non-Hispanic whites,
12.8 percent for non-Hispanic blacks, and 22.1 percent for Hispanics.

A close look at occupational distribution indicates that
although Dominicans continued to be overrepresented in blue-
collar manufacturing jobs in 1990, during the 1980s they lost a
solid 15.9 percent in that job market (see table 4.3). Also,
besides their modest increase of 7.3 percent in middle and low
white-collar jobs (technical, sales, and clerical) from 1980 to

TABLE 4.3 **Occupational Distribution of the Labor Force, New York City, 1990**
         (Persons 16 years of age or older, in %)

Occupation	Non-HW	Non-HB	Hispanic	Dominican
Managerial and professional	38.5	19.6	13.9	9.6%
Technical, sales, and admnistrative support	35.6	36.6	30.9	27.1
Service workers	10.1	24.0	23.1	22.5
Farming, forestry, and fishing	0.4	0.4	0.6	0.4
Precision product, craft, and repair	7.8	6.6	9.4	9.6
Operators, fabircators, and laborers	7.6	12.8	22.1	30.9

SOURCE: Hernández, Rivera-Batiz, and Agodini 1995.

1990, they did not obtain any significant gain in any of the occupational categories in the service sector. Thus, contrary to the claim that immigrants are needed for a variety of blue-collar and low-skilled jobs generated within the service economy, we found that among Dominicans the loss of blue-collar and unskilled jobs in the manufacturing sector has not been offset by a proportionate gain of jobs in the service sector. Instead, we see that their significant loss of shares in manufacturing combined with their modest gain in the service sector during the 1980s affected their labor force participation rates and levels of employment.

Earnings

Defined as the sum of wage or salary income, farm and non-farm earnings do not tell us much unless they are compared with prices and against other earnings within a given society. While the analysis of purchasing power and earnings was addressed in chapter 3, this section starts with the question of how, compared to other groups, Dominicans are doing in terms of earnings. Implicit in that question is the need to assess the value ascribed to Dominican immigrant workers. The answer to it may bring us closer to understanding the meaning of cheap labor and the place of low-wage workers in an advanced capitalist economy.

Data on the distribution of earnings show that throughout the three periods covered, compared to the other ethnic groups, Dominicans had the lowest earnings. Similarly, during the 1980s, the earning gap between both Dominican men and women and the highest earners (non-Hispanic whites) became wider. After adjusting for inflation, in 1989 the average annual earnings of Dominican males was $15,139 while non-Hispanic whites earned $36,272, non-Hispanic blacks, $20,707, and Hispanics, $18,540. While in 1989 the average annual earnings of a Dominican male worker increased by $1,157, the annual earnings of a non-Hispanic white male worker increased by $7,619, reflecting an earning gap in 1989 of $21,133, compared to 1979 when the gap had been $14,671. That is to say that in 1979 Dominican males earned 48.7 cents per every dollar earned by a non-Hispanic white male. In 1989 the distance between the two groups became wider when this earning was reduced to 41.7 cents per dollar.

In 1989 the earning gap between Dominican men and Hispanic men was slightly reduced. In 1979 the average Dominican male earned 78 cents per every dollar earned by the average Hispanic male, and in 1989 that earning increased to 81 cents per every dollar. It should be noted, however, that the reduction of that gap does not correspond to high earning increase for Dominican males, but it was due, rather, to the fact that the annual earnings of Hispanic males, compared to other male workers, experienced the lowest increase, or a change of only 3.5 percent, between 1979 and 1989.

Dominican women on their part exhibit significantly lower annual earnings compared to other women in the city. Relative to non-Hispanic white women, the earnings of Dominican women reflect an even wider gap between 1979 and 1989. After adjusting for inflation, in 1989 the average annual earnings for Dominican women was $11,371, compared to non-Hispanic white women who on the average earned $23,521, non-Hispanic black women, $18,695, and Hispanic women, $14,553. As table 4.4 indicates, in 1989 the average annual earnings of Dominican women increased modestly from $10,007 to $11,371, substantially below those of non-Hispanic white women, whose earnings increased from $17,411 to $23,521. If in 1979 a Dominican woman earned 57.4 cents per every dollar earned by a non-Hispanic white woman, this earning was reduced in 1989 to 48.3 cents.

Labor Force Participation Rates and Unemployment

Labor force participation, defined as the ratio of the active labor force to the total prime working age population, is frequently used to estimate the size and composition of labor reserves. Table 4.5 shows labor force participation rates by sex and ethnic/racial origin. In 1980, among the groups compared, Dominican men had the highest labor force participation rate

TABLE 4.4 **Changes in Annual Earnings in New York City, 1979, 1989, 1997**
(*Employed persons 16 years of age or older*)

Population	1979 Earnings (in $)	1980-1990 Earnings	% Change
MEN			
Dominican	13,982	15,139	8.3
New York City overall	25,141	28,815	14.6
Non-Hispanic white	28,653	36,272	26.6
Non-Hispanic black	19,410	20,703	8.2
Hispanic overall	17,908	18,540	3.5
WOMEN			
Dominican	10,007	11,371	13.6
New York City overall	16,304	20,425	25.3
Non-Hispanic white	17,411	23,521	35.1
Non-Hispanic black	15,566	18,695	20.1
Hispanic overall	12,611	14,553	15.4

SOURCE: Hernández, Rivera-Batiz, and Agodini 1995.

with 73.1 percent. The corresponding numbers for non-Hispanic white men was 71.1 percent, for non-Hispanic black men, 65.0 percent, and for Hispanic men overall, 70.6 percent.

Dominican and Hispanic women had almost similar labor force participation rates, or 49.1 percent and 49.2 percent respectively. But compared to non-Hispanic white women, who had 53.3 percent, non-Hispanic black women, who had 60.2 percent, and women in general, who had 54.6 percent, Dominican females had significantly lower participation rates in the labor force.

It is important to note that during the 1980s and the 1990s, the labor force participation rates of Dominican men was negatively affected. As indicated in table 4.5, compared to 1980, Dominican men lost shares in 1990 and 1997. In addition, among the ethnic groups compared here, Dominican males were the only ones who experienced a decline of 2.5 percent in their participation rate in the labor force in 1990. The others experienced moderate increases, ranging from 1.3 percent to 2.8 percent.

On their part, compared to 1980, Dominican women experienced a slight increase of 1.8 percent in labor force participation rates, but their increase lagged substantially behind other women, who experienced increases ranging from 5.8 percent for non-Hispanic white women to 8.3 percent for non-Hispanic

TABLE 4.5 **Labor Force Participation Rates, New York City, 1980, 1990, 1997**
(Persons 16 years of age or older)

POPULATION GROUP	Labor Force Participation Rate (%)					
	MALE			FEMALE		
	1980	1990	1997	1980	1990	1997
Dominican	75.6	73.1	60.7	47.3	49.1	42.4
New York City	70.5	71.8	68.3	47.8	54.6	50.8
Non-Hispanic white	71.8	72.4	70.0	47.5	53.3	52.7
Non-Hispanic black	65.0	67.8	61.3	51.9	60.2	50.5
Hispanic overall	70.6	72.6	67.9	41.2	49.2	44.1

SOURCE: For 1980 and 1990, Hernández, Rivera-Batiz, and Agodini 1995; for 1997, Hernández and Rivera-Batiz 1997.

black women. In 1980 Dominican women had a higher labor force participation rate (47.3%) than Hispanic women in general (41.2%), but in 1990, due to the disparity in the increases both groups experienced, Hispanic women were able to reduce the gap and slightly surpass Dominican women, moving to 49.2 percent. Similarly, while in 1980 Dominican women almost equaled the labor force participation rates of women overall in the city (47.3 percent for Dominicans and 47.8 percent for New York City women), in 1990 women in New York City increased their shares over Dominicans by 5.5 percent.

While some may argue that variations in labor force participation rates can be attributed to general tendencies in the economy, particularly to cyclical ups and downs, in the case of Dominican men, however, the overall declines in labor force participation rates, particularly the precipitous drop of 1997, seems to reflect more the dynamics of structural tendencies in the city's economy, such as the absolute decline of employment in specific labor markets. Similarly, while in the particular case of Dominican women their low participation rates in the labor force is consistent with that of Hispanic women, who tend to have lower labor force participation rates than non-Hispanic white women and particularly non-Hispanic black women, in the case of Dominican men, their drastic drop in labor force participation in 1997 brings them closer to non-Hispanic blacks, who, throughout 1980 and 1990 held the lowest participation rates among the groups compared.

Table 4.6 indicates unemployment rates by sex for the various ethnic groups compared. It shows that with the exception of Hispanic males, who actually reduced their unemployment rate in 1990, from 14.0 percent to 12.4 percent, other males experienced small increases. A similar pattern can be seen in 1997, when unemployment figures maintained more or less similar values, with the exception of Dominicans and non-Hispanic blacks, who experienced moderate increases, ranging from 3.7 to 3.8 percent. It should be noted, however, that among the male groups, Dominican males exhibited the highest unemployment rates for the three periods.

In the case of working women, with the exception of non-Hispanic white females, who experienced a decline in their unemployment rates in 1990, unemployment rates increased for the rest of the women in this study, reflecting 18.4 percent for Dominicans, 8.1 percent for New York City women overall, 10.9 for non-Hispanic blacks, and 13.6 percent for Hispanics. Note that while Dominican women almost doubled their unemployment rate from 1980 to 1990, that is from 9.5 percent to 18.4 percent, other women experienced only slight increases, ranging from 1.0 percent for non-Hispanic blacks to 1.4 percent for New York City women overall. As with men, unemployment rates among all women groups increased slightly in 1997 but remained extremely high for Dominican women.

Explaining Labor Market Differentiations

Several explanations have been offered to account for labor market differences among workers. The explanations could be divided into two groups: those dealing with supply and those dealing with demand. While supply theories focus on workers' abilities, skills, quantity, as well as demographic factors such as age, marital status, and the like, demand theories focus on the host country's economy, its structural changes, and its needs.[4]

TABLE 4.6 **Unemployment Rates in New York City, 1980, 1990, 1997**
(Persons 16 years of age or older)

| POPULATION GROUP | Unemployment Rate in % | | | | | |
| | MALE | | | FEMALE | | |
	1980	1990	1997	1980	1990	1997
Dominican	14.3	15.1	18.9	9.5	18.4	18.6
New York City	7.0	8.7	10.3	6.6	8.1	9.0
Non-Hispanic white	5.0	5.5	7.1	5.1	4.9	5.9
Non-Hispanic black	13.1	14.3	18.0	9.9	10.9	13.6
Hispanic overall	14.0	12.4	12.6	12.2	13.6	12.0

SOURCE: For 1980 and 1990, Hernández, Rivera-Batiz, and Agodini 1995; for 1997, Hernández and Rivera-Batiz 1997.

On theories focusing on supply understood as a set of variables, including educational attainment, job experience, training, and skills, human capital has been found to play an important role in establishing labor market differences among workers. In explaining labor market outcomes among immigrants, George Borjas concludes that "when unskilled immigrants enter the labor force, they are likely to have difficulty finding and holding on to a job. . . . Hence low wage or unskilled immigrant groups will have relatively high unemployment rates" (1990:136). In a consequent study of immigrants in the United States, using the Public Use Samples of the U.S. Population Census from 1940 to 1980, Borjas (1992) examined levels of skills and found that postwar immigrants, who had poor skill levels and low educational attainment, also had poor labor market outcomes, as reflected in their high unemployment, low earnings, lower labor force participation, and weak attachment to the labor market. On their part, K. McCarthy and R. Burciaga Valdez found that low earnings among Mexican immigrants was connected to their low educational attainment, particularly to their persistent failure to increase the number of college graduates among Mexican-American generations (1985).

A useful contribution to the human capital debate is provided by economist Francisco Rivera-Batiz (1991), who aptly argues that years of schooling alone do not properly explain wage differences among workers. For example, Rivera-Batiz contends that quality of schooling could generate different educational skills. Preferring to examine literacy (academic knowledge in English reading and quantitative skills), he has posited that "the statistical analysis unequivocally suggests that literacy skills are a major variable explaining wage differentials among Hispanics" (71).

On the demand side, scholars have found that economic structural changes have led to earning differences among workers through the specific creation of less-valued jobs. The shifting of the economy from manufacturing to services, for instance, replaced well-paying and stable blue-collar manufacturing jobs with low-paying blue-collar service jobs. In one of the most clear and coherent statements presented to date about the nature of employment in the United States, Bennett Harrison and Barry Bluestone have shown that economic restructuring combined with government policies have pushed this country into a "great U turn" in which "the decade of the 1980s . . . bore a credible resemblance to the 1920s" (Harrison and Bluestone 1988:viii). The authors state that since the 1960s, the United States has turned into a service society characterized by growing poverty, too few well-paying jobs, and an abundance of jobs of "dubious quality."

An important variable among demand-side theories is the geographical location of workers and job growth. Residential patterns, for instance, have been found to have an effect in the labor market outcomes of blacks. John Kasarda's (1983; 1990) well-known studies on employment and blacks found that in some metropolitan cities, economic restructuring produced a mismatch between jobs and black workers. High rates of job-lessness, declined earnings, and poverty among blacks corre-sponded to the fact that black workers, though needing entry-level and low educational–level jobs, resided in urban areas where these jobs were being replaced by jobs demanding higher educational levels. At the same time, jobs that required low educational levels were growing in the suburbs, but they were geographically removed from the urban centers where unskilled black workers were concentrated.

Poor Labor Market Outcomes Among Dominicans: Current Explanations

The discussion presented thus far could partially explain poor labor market outcomes among Dominican workers. There is evidence that Dominicans have low educational attainment, high proportions of blue-collar and unskilled workers, and lim-ited English proficiency. They also tend to reside almost exclu-sively in urban areas.

The underrepresentation of Dominicans in upper white-collar occupations is connected to their low educational attainment. Similarly, their limited English proficiency affects their likelihood to move to middle and low white-collar occupations, as well as the public sector. Table 4.7 presents the educational levels of Dominicans in New York City compared to other ethnic groups, as well as the overall population of the city. It shows that Dominicans had the highest proportion of persons twenty-five years of age or older who had not completed high school. Both in 1990, as well as in 1997, as many as 52.3 percent and 54.7 percent respectively of Dominicans twenty-five years of age or older had less than a highschool education. The corresponding number for the overall population of New York City were 20.8 percent and 24.1 percent, for non-Hispanic whites, 11.7 percent and 12.0 percent, for non-Hispanic blacks, 24.9 percent and 25.5 percent, and for Hispanics, 40.4 percent and 48.4 percent. On the other hand, among the groups compared, Dominicans had the smallest representation among people twenty-five years of age or older who had completed college or higher. In 1997, only 4.0 percent of Dominicans had completed college or more, compared to 26.8 percent for the overall population of the city, 40.2 percent for non-Hispanic whites, 12.8 percent of non-Hispanic blacks, and 8.8 percent of Hispanics.

TABLE 4.7 **The Educational Status of the Population in New York City, 1990 and 1997** *(Persons 25 years of age or older)*

	Percentage of the Population Completing:							
POPULATION GROUP	*LESS THAN HIGH SCHOOL*		*HIGH SCHOOL*		*SOME COLLEGE*		*COLLEGE OR MORE*	
	1990	*1996*	*1990*	*1996*	*1990*	*1996*	*1990*	*1997*
Dominican	52.3	54.7	20.4	25.0	19.3	16.3	8.0	4.0
NYC	20.8	24.1	24.8	31.5	24.5	17.6	29.9	26.8
Non-HW	11.7	12.0	23.2	29.8	23.5	18.0	41.6	40.2
Non-HB	24.9	25.5	29.9	39.7	29.6	22.0	15.6	12.8
Hispanic	40.4	48.4	25.6	28.4	23.1	15.2	10.9	8.0

SOURCE: For 1980 and 1990, Hernández, Rivera-Batiz, and Agodini 1995; for 1997, Hernández and Rivera-Batiz, 1997.

As indicated in table 4.8, during the 1980s foreign-born Dominicans made significant progress in their educational levels. In 1980 a total of 72.0 percent of Dominicans twenty-five years of age or older had less than a high school education. In 1990 this total was reduced to 52.2 percent. In contrast, U.S.-born Dominicans with similar characteristics were less fortunate, experiencing a moderate drop from 35.0 percent to 30.6 percent. Similarly, foreign-born Dominicans more than doubled the total of those who had completed college or more, from 3.5 percent to 7.5 percent, but U.S.-born Dominicans experienced a decline in this category, from 16.7 percent to 12.2 percent.

The educational progress experienced by foreign-born Dominicans, reflected in an increase in the years of schooling, is associated with the constant influx of immigrants coming from the Dominican Republic, which accelerated during the 1980s, reflecting a more diverse demographic profile. In 1970, for instance, 16.8 percent of Dominicans admitted to the United States reported upper, intermediate, and low-skilled white-collar occupations. But for those admitted from 1982 to 1989, these occupations represented a total of 24.7 percent.[5] Yet, years of schooling, as Rivera-Batiz has argued, have been offset by low levels of English literacy among foreign-born Dominicans, who in 1990, as much as 47.3 percent were unable

TABLE 4.8 **Changes in Educational Attainment of U.S.-Born and Immigrant Dominicans, 1990 (*Persons 25 years of age or older*)**

POPULATION GROUP	Percentage of the Population Completing:			
	LESS THAN HIGH SCHOOL		HIGH SCHOOL OR SOME COLLEGE	COLLEGE OR MORE
Dominican immigrants	1980	72.7	23.8	3.5
	1990	54.3	38.2	7.5
U.S.-born Dominicans	1980	35.0	48.3	16.7
	1990	30.6	57.2	12.2

SOURCE: Hernández, Rivera-Batiz, and Agodini 1995.

to speak English or spoke it poorly (see figure 6). U.S.-born Dominicans, on the other hand, represent a young population, whose low educational outcomes result from increasing high rates of school dropouts and other related problems affecting their school districts.

It is likely that residential patterns may have also affected labor market outcomes among Dominican workers. As indicated previously, the overwhelming majority of Dominicans reside in New York City. Although the percentage of Dominicans settling in New York City has declined since the 1970s, in 1997 a solid 69.1 percent of total Dominicans residing in the United States claimed this city as their home. On the other hand, job growth, particularly blue-collar and low-skilled service jobs, was highest in the suburbs and their intermediate and outer areas, which are distant from Dominican settlements. "Between 1978 and 1989, for example, employment in grocery retailing in New York and New Jersey suburbs increased by 25 percent. But in New York's outer boroughs it increased by less than 1 percent" (O'Neill and Moss 1991:57). Similarly, while wholesale employment in Manhattan experienced an absolute loss of 27,300 jobs, the outlying suburbs had an absolute gain of 28,100 wholesale jobs (52). The fact that more than 20 percent of Dominican homes did not own a telephone in 1990 and that public transportation to and from these regions is expensive contributed to isolate Dominicans further from areas of high job growth.

The shifting of the economy from manufacturing to service and the increasing loss of well-paying blue-collar, unskilled jobs had a devastating effect on Dominican immigrants, who are mostly unskilled, blue-collar workers. During the 1980s, for instance, among all the Caribbean nations, the Dominican Republic had the highest proportion of unskilled, blue-collar workers admitted to New York City. From 1982 to 1989, 36.6 percent of those Dominicans were classified as operators, fabricators, and laborers. The corresponding proportion for the entire Caribbean region, excluding the Dominican Republic, was 21.4 percent.[6]

**Toward an Alternative Explanation Concerning Labor Market
Outcomes Among Dominicans**

Labor force participation among Dominicans was relatively
high during the 1970s, due perhaps to the relative low volume
of migration and the momentary need for workers caused by
the socioeconomic change taking place in the manufacturing
sector. For example, there is great variation in the mean annual
admission of immigrants from the Dominican Republic from
1966 to 1985: 12,579 in the first decade (1966 to 1975) and
18,316 in the second (1976 to 1985). Their increasing and constant migration, combined with the arrival of other groups who
were attracted to the same job market, could have created a
state of saturation, particularly in a market that was the product
of a volatile moment of economic restructuring. That demographic dynamic could have also led to labor substitution.[7]

Regarding labor substitution and industrial restructuring,
Torres and Bonilla argue that the reorganization of industrial
production into light manufacturing during the 1970s led,
once again, to the displacement of Puerto Rican workers. The
recomposed manufacturing sector in New York City was reor-
ganized on the basis of a reduction of production costs, particularly labor. New immigrants, unskilled and desperate to work,
became the ideal labor force for the sector (1993:101). Thus,
economic transformations, particularly those caused by the
need to reduce the cost of production, lead to a relative shortage of labor. In this case, then, it is not that workers willingly
withdrew from the labor market as some scholars have suggested about some sectors of the native working class; rather, as
argued by Torres and Bonilla, they are simply rejected and substituted in the process of capitalist production.

Similarly, the process of reorganization in manufacturing
production, as with any other productive change, involved a
number of transitional stages (from definition and technological changes to market orientation) and attracted a good number of new workers. The kind of commitment to workers in this
new labor market would become clear as the process devel-

oped, particularly as permitted by the elasticity of demand once the new markets were stable.

Once the new markets became relatively stable, the elasticity of their demand began to be affected, as was reflected in the constant drop in the number of people employed or in their anemic growth. Take, for instance, the manufacturing sector. As figure 7 shows, the number of jobs in this sector has fallen precipitously since the 1960s, without adding enough new jobs to replace the ones eliminated. That is to say that the development of new manufacturing jobs (regardless of their conditions, i.e., downgraded or low-paying) has occurred within a shrinking process, which, to this moment, seems to be irreversible. Similarly, as the graph shows, in spite of its remarkable expansion, the growth of service jobs has not been evenly distributed within the service sector. From 1960 to 1990, the growth of jobs in retail trade, for instance, has been negative, declining from 12.19 percent to 10.80 percent. The dynamic areas of the service industries (i.e., finance, insurance, and real estate) forced by global competition experienced profound changes, including downsizing, mergers, and acquisitions, resulting in large labor cuts. At the national level, between 1980 and 1987, Fortune 500 companies reduced their labor force by 3.1 million jobs (Christesen et al. 1994).

The direct reduction of jobs, particularly of high-paying jobs within the FIRE industries, had a negative impact in those jobs, whether formal or informal, that had developed to satisfy the needs and specificities of a high-paying clientele. Job reduction, besides limiting the multiplying effects of high-income jobs, and the reorganization of labor, particularly in small firms in New York City, have led to further reduction in the use of labor. In fact, in a recent study of contingent workers in small and medium-size firms in New York City, it was found that 98 percent of all firms in the city had less than 100 workers and that 31 percent of them worked specifically in manufacturing, business, and financial services. More importantly, the study found that many of these firms in seeking to reduce the cost of production were planning to move their production elsewhere.

Regarding the use of labor in the city, the authors conclude that "the number of core, permanent employees in many firms is shrinking. . . . The smaller the firms the more likely they are to use contingent staffing as a powerful lever to maximize profits" (Christesen et al. 1994:44).

The Limits of Demand

Traditionally, migrant workers have been understood as the expression of an exodus of surplus labor that moves to areas that are expected to offer employment opportunities. Since they moved in search of employment, it seemed inconceivable that they would consciously invest time or money in a journey that promised no reward. Yet some scholars have recently began to note that modern societies, particularly those with high immigrant flows, have witnessed a growing disparity between jobs and job seekers. The disparity, normally associated with specific job markets and workers within a given economy, is being increasingly understood as a structural tendency that affects all kinds of wage workers regardless of their human capital stock, position in the labor market, or nativity. Thus the pool of unused workers increases through direct unemployment, resulting from increased lay-offs and/or the adding of new job seekers who are unable to find employment, as well as through a fall in the labor force resulting from discouraged workers and/or potential workers who are absorbed at educational centers.[8]

In *Beyond Employment: Time, Work, and the Informal Economy*, Claus Offe and Rolf Heinze (1992) argue that in advanced societies wage work is turning more and more into a precious stone that fewer people possess. Increasing unemployment levels, they argue, show us "that 'being employed' is not really the normal state of affairs; people only think it is" (1). Instead, "the normal state of affairs" is growing unemployment, part-time work, shorter work weeks, multi earner households, and an informal economy.

The rise of the service economy has been generally understood as a job market capable of absorbing a growing labor force. It was widely accepted that services generated a variety of highly skilled, low-skilled, white-collar, and blue-collar jobs. Unlike modern manufacturing, service industries are relatively labor intensive; they require a greater use of labor relative to capital resources. But the service economy has been severely criticized for its inability to produce well-paying jobs to replace long-gone old manufacturing jobs, for its propensity to create systematic economic slowdowns through increasing the cost of labor (through enhancing human capital) without increasing its productivity, and, most crucial to our argument, for its incapacity to produce enough jobs to satisfy the employment needs of a growing labor force.

In *The Jobless Future: Sci-Tech and the Dogma of Work*, sociologists Stanley Aronowitz and Willian DiFazio (1994) present the problem of not having enough jobs as being pervasive in modern capitalist society. They argue that the United States is characterized today by a productive process that increasingly displaces workers and generates unemployment, underemployment, and low-paying jobs. The authors argue against the belief that displaced workers in advanced societies are somehow reincorporated into the process of production, and that semiskilled and highly skilled workers were protected from facing replacement and unemployment in the labor process (Aronowitz and DiFazio 1994:326–27). They point out that "all of the contradictory tendencies involved in the restructuring of global capital and computer-mediated work seem to lead to the same conclusion for workers of all collars—that is unemployment, underemployment, decreasingly skilled work, and relatively lower wages. These sci-tech transformations of the labor process have disrupted the workplace and workers' community and culture. The new technology will destroy more jobs than it creates. The new technology has fewer parts and fewer workers and produces more products. This is true not only in traditional production industries but for all workers, including managers and technical workers" (3).

Today capitalists have found new ways to accumulate without increasing their use of human labor, thereby helping to augment the labor reserve. Harry Magdoff complained about the lack of discussion concerning the working class in a world more and more controlled by competition, less commodity production, and, particularly, growing accumulation through financial transactions involving international banks. He felt that investors were moving freely in search of lower wages, and that "factories that decide not to move will be motivated to reduce labor cost by modernization that will eliminate jobs. Both of these developments create a real threat to the working classes of nations already burdened by mass unemployment" (1989:360).

Offe and Heinze (1992) explain, for instance, that today more and more consumers are falling into what they call "Do It Yourself," (DIY). The authors conclude that the basic idea behind DIY is simply to save money by using one's own energy and knowledge. A tendency that we have witnessed in New York City is that consumers can presumably lower the price of a given product by buying it unassembled and carrying it home. As a result, consumers are no longer merely consumers at a given moment in time. Now they may simultaneously be consumers, nonwage delivery people, and nonwage assemblers. In the transformation process, however, at least two workers have been directly displaced.

It is interesting to note that although retail sales in New York City, after being stagnant since 1988, increased by 2.9 percent in 1994. The growth, however, did not translate into job gains in the sector. While employment grew by 1.9 percent in eating and drinking establishments, mostly as a result of increases in the number of tourists, merchandise stores, where today more and more unassembled products are being sold, employment fell by 8.3 percent, affecting the net total of job growth in the retail sector (McCall and Scanlon 1995:27–28).

In a recent study on employment in fast-food establishments in central Harlem conducted by a team from Columbia University, it was found that "inner-city fast-food jobs have become the object of fierce competition. The ratio of job applicants to hires is about 14 to 1. . . . Jobs once considered solely the province of high school drop-outs or young people starting out in the work world are now dominated by workers in their mid- and late 20s who are trying to support families on $4.25 an hour—$170 a week" (Newman 1995:23).

During the past two decades, the position of Dominican workers in the labor market has decayed progressively. In 1980, for instance, compared to the other ethnic groups, Dominicans had higher or equal labor force participation rates while keeping the highest unemployment levels and the lowest earnings. During the 1980s and 1990s, however, their position deteriorated. During these periods, Dominicans not only continued to experience the highest unemployment rates and the lowest earnings, but their labor force participation rate, particularly among males, was severely affected. It is important to note also that during these years, Dominican males reduced their labor force participation rate precisely at a moment when every other group experienced increases. What remains to be seen is whether the present labor market conditions among Dominicans reflect the making of a Dominican underclass in New York City, particularly since their labor market outcomes are very similar to that of non-Hispanic blacks. As discussed in the following chapter, among the Hispanic groups compared, Dominicans in New York City have, by far, the highest percentage of people who classified themselves as "black."

If, as we have shown, the tendency has been to reduce the use of labor in some job markets, and the experience of Dominican workers does not leave one much room to think of them as workers who have somehow managed to circumvent the pervasive trends in the receiving society, how can one argue soundly that current migration flows to the United States from the Dominican Republic, or anywhere else for that matter, is a direct respond to the need for workers in the host society? The answer to this question is not in a hidden demand for labor in some underground new market whose elasticity knows no limits. To the contrary, increasing, well-articulated, and systematic attacks against immigrants emanating from various quarters of government and sectors of civil society clearly indicate that new foreign hands, particularly poor and unskilled, are no longer needed nor wanted here. In this sense, the continued influx of immigrants to the United States does not necessarily respond to a need of the receiving society. As explained in chapter 1, it could more conceivably respond to the needs of the sending society and, ultimately, to the needs of the migrants themselves.

5.

ON THE INTERNATIONAL MOBILITY OF LABOR

Two theoretical paradigms are normally offered to explain the international mobility of workers: the equilibrium model and the historical-structural model. The equilibrium model is rooted in John Stuart Mill's concept of order and balance and in Max Weber's concept of rationalization. Mill believed in the power that certain forces had to prevent chaos and generate stability and balance in society. War and disease, for instance, serve to check the excessive growth of the population. At the same time, the opening of new markets and adjusting production to the capacity of the market facilitate the regulation of commodity production to the level of demand (Mill 1900:153—56 vol. I; 75–82 vol. II). Similarly, the emigration of those who cannot find employment in their native land, costing the sending society nothing, prevents people from being "wasted at home in reckless speculations" (366 vol. I). In Mill's view, the redistribution of population from an overcrowded area to one in need of workers represented more than economic convenience or individual motive. He believed that the encouragement of migration by the State generated benefits to both the sending society and the receiving society by bringing about equilibrium in the redistribution of people and resources (470–80 vol. II).

Max Weber's typology of social actions, encapsulated in the term *Zweckrational* (instrumental action), is the conceptual layer to the equilibrium model. Weber highlighted rational praxis, steps taken under the assumption of a deliberate pursuit of goals based on the calculation of the cost, efficiency, and benefits involved (Weber 1978:24–26 vol. I). Weber thought of modern society as being characterized by the expansion of the use of rationality, or the spread of purposeful reason. He was convinced that individual and institutional actions, economic or otherwise, increasingly stemmed from an understanding of clear goals with specified benefits and costs. The mobility of workers from one arena to another is to be seen, therefore, as a function of the instrumental action that Weber ascribes to human behavior in society.[1]

Conversely, the historical-structural model, which is largely a reaction to the equilibrium approach, can be traced to Karl Marx and Friedrich Engels's understanding of historical events from a socioeconomic point of view. Marx and Engels believed that as productive forces changed in a given society, all other social institutions (politics, law, religion, art, etc.) would change accordingly (Marx and Engels 1978). According to this logic, population movements are seen as being part of a totality of changes affecting the process of production in a given society. In their view, emigration from Ireland in the nineteenth century did not result from overpopulation, as many believed. Emigration from Ireland was compulsory and represented a social phenomenon experienced in many parts of the world during different historical stages; it was triggered by socioeconomic imperatives. Marx and Engels argued that modern forced emigration stemmed from changes introduced in the process of production, "produced by landlorism, concentration of farms, application of machinery to the soil, and introduction of the modern system of agriculture on a great scale. . . . It [was] not population that presse[d] on productive power; it [was] productive power that presse[d] on population" (Marx and Engels 1975:56–57).

Migration scholars who are proponents of the equilibrium

model start from a micro perspective. The potential migrant is perceived as a *rational* agent who chooses to move on the basis of clear calculations of the cost and benefits involved in migrating. For migrant workers, the prospects of getting better jobs and wages in the host country become the dominant factor behind their decision to move (Harris and Todaro 1970; Sjaastad 1962). By the same token, their move generates a state of balance, or equilibrium, with regard to the two localities involved in the migratory process by removing excess labor from one setting to satisfy the need for workers in another (Spengler and Meyers 1977). Seen from this point of view, migration becomes a favorable "win-win" arrangement for all parties concerned.

Proponents of the historical-structural approach, on the other hand, assume a less harmonious macroview of society. They presuppose that some workers move due to the pressure of socioeconomic changes generated in the production system that impact the use of and need for laborers in the home country (History Task Force 1979; Bonilla and Campos 1981). Within this logic, forced migration corresponds to the dynamic of uneven capitalist economic development and the movement of global capitalism (Emmanuel 1972; Amin 1974; Portes 1978). From the perspective of such a framework, the relocation of surplus laborers, which is often orchestrated by the governments of the sending and receiving societies, stems from a demand for cheap labor in the host locality. Thus, while the equilibrium perspective assumes that migrant workers would move only if they can attain a better deal than what their native society has to offer, the historical-structural model suggests that the spatial location and distribution of workers depend on changes in the productive system.

These are opposing conceptual tendencies whose dissimilar character lies in the essence of their propositions. One is centered on the agency of the individual who migrates in order to satisfy his personal needs; the other is centered on forces that emanate from society's mode of production, which explains the reasons behind a group of people's urge to move. While both theoretical paradigms may start from different propositions regarding the role of the individual in the migratory process, they do not disagree about the reasons behind a receiving society's willingness to receive migrants. While they differ in presenting the way workers may embark on a migratory journey, either by their own initiative or in response to invisible forces beyond their control, the two theories seem to share the understanding that workers will relocate to areas where a need for their labor exists. Both theoretical paradigms enjoy the support of numerous scholars.[2] In the following section, we will look closely at the point of convergence for the two theories in question, that is, the mobility of workers vis-à-vis the presumed need for laborers in the receiving society.

Labor Mobility and Demand

In the equilibrium model, workers take the initiative to move from society A to society B because they expect to gain material benefits by finding a better job or earning higher wages. In the historical-structural model, workers relocate from society A, where they have become part of the surplus labor force, to society B, where they can reenter the process of production and generate surplus value. Both theories construe relocation as potentially productive to both the migrants and the receiving society. Migrants expect a better job, higher wages, or simply reincorporation into the labor process. For the receiving society, the movement promises to address labor shortages or, more importantly, to provide a cheaper supply of workers. Both theories uphold the conception of a correlation between supply and demand in the labor market of the host country. This logic presents international labor migration as the result of two combined variables: the workers' need to emigrate due to their home country's inability to employ them and the host country's interest in a cheaper labor force.

The understanding of international migration as the result of a demand for cheap labor by the host country presupposes the existence of jobs awaiting migrants in the host society. By implication, this reasoning overlooks the possibility of unwanted immigration. Similarly, marginalization and long-standing poverty among immigrants, resulting from high rates of unemployment and underemployment in receiving societies, would insinuate a more complex paradigm. The study of Dominican migrants in New York City lends itself to an exploration of the aforementioned assumptions. As previously discussed, Dominican immigrants exhibit persistent high levels of poverty and marginalization, welfare dependency, unemployment and underemployment upon their arrival. The fact that everyone who came looking for a job was not able to find one suggests that a migratory movement may not necessarily reflect the need for workers by the receiving society. In other words, the society that received the workers may not need or want them.

The link between labor migration and labor demand also suggests that a society's lack of interest in foreign workers would be enough to deter potential job seekers from reaching its shores. Yet persistent reports concerning the increasing influx of immigrants into nations, which since World War II have maintained restrictive immigration policies, would indicate the difficulty of preventing and regulating the entrance of unwanted visitors. Current evidence seem to suggest that immigration may persist in spite of a nation's position against it. Within the past few years, for instance, Germany, England, Italy, and Japan have proposed new laws against the increasing immigration of Eastern Europeans, North Africans, Middle Easterners, and South Asians. Among some countries, the idea to create a common immigration law under the European Community to bar the door to unwanted immigration has gained currency, while other nations have gone as far as imposing high monetary sanctions on airlines that bring in undocumented migrants. In Puerto Rico, alarmed by the increasing number of Dominicans who, uninvited, arrive daily on the island, some high-ranking authorities have publicly suggested the idea of charging the Dominican government a specified amount of money per every undocumented Dominican apprehended in Puerto Rico.

Migration and Declining Labor Demand at the Core

The arrival of Dominicans in the United States coincided with a declining demand for blue-collar and unskilled workers, as well as the mass entrance of other immigrants who were attracted to the job market. Coming mostly from Asia, Latin America, and the Caribbeans, immigrants tended to concentrate in large metropolitan cities, where they expected to find entry-level jobs. During the 1970s and 1980s, along with thousands of Dominicans, thousands of other immigrants, particularly Hispanics and West Indians, settled in New York City. The city was then experiencing an economic transformation that radically changed the needs of the labor market. The industrial-based economy began to be replaced by a high-tech and service oriented economy. Native low- and unskilled blue-collar workers, particularly from ethnic minorities, could not withstand the high unemployment levels and declining industrial demand. They began to abandon the city in droves, while large numbers of immigrants, expecting to find jobs, began to enter. By 1990, despite the large immigration influx, New York City still had almost one million people less than it had in 1960. Yet, the mobility of people had noticeably changed the demographic composition of the city.

I

The declining demand for blue-collar and unskilled workers and the increasing influx of immigrants would have serious negative repercussions for all city workers searching for unskilled jobs. The combination of declining demand and a growing supply of workers posessing similar skills would generate competition among job seekers, native and foreign born, resulting in their easy substitution by employers. The works of

Frank Bonilla and Ricardo Campos on Puerto Rican workers have pointed to a process of labor substitution that is provoked by the mobility of capital and labor. Economic transformations in Puerto Rico and in the United States displaced thousands of Puerto Rican low- and unskilled workers, who were mobilized within the Caribbean and North American geographies, which Bonilla and Campos view as one single labor market. But while jobless Puerto Ricans had to move back and forth between their island homeland and the mainland searching for scarce unskilled jobs, new immigrants arrived in both places, looking to compete for the same scarce jobs that Puerto Ricans were pursuing. Similarly, while thousands of Puerto Ricans remained jobless, many of the new arrivals would accommodate themselves to the same economies that had driven the former out (Bonilla and Campos 1981;1986).

Scholars have also suggested that the increasing immigration of unskilled workers affected the wages of unskilled native workers. George Borjas, Richard B. Freeman, and Lawrence F. Katz, among others, have measured the effects of large groups of immigrants on the labor force. Analyzing demographic data from the 1980 census, current population surveys, export and import figures, and employment rates of large manufacturing industries, these authors found that the combination of immigration and trade deficits reduced the employment opportunities for less skilled native workers and caused a decrease of between 30 to 50 percent in their wages (Borjas, Freeman, and Katz 1992:215). Trade flows are negatively affected by the fact that import industries employ relatively fewer skilled workers, many of whom are underpaid immigrants. The authors argue that the effects of immigration on the work force should be understood as long-lasting, because "unlike trade deficits that change the implicit labor supply only annually, immigration increases the nation's work force permanently (as long as immigrants remain economically active)" (214).

While some scholars have doubted the negative effects of immigration on opportunities in the labor market and wages of native workers, there is consensus in the literature concerning its negative impacts on the labor market outcomes of immigrants.[3] New arrivals provide employers with bargaining power against longtime immigrants who have managed to gain employment and secure some benefits. In a study of immigrant workers in Ventura County, California, Richard Mines and Phillip L. Martin found that "while the more recent migrants caused displacement, the displaced workers [were] not American citizens. Rather, the jobs of other Mexicans [were] being threatened" (Mines and Martin 1984:138–39). Mexican workers, who had relatively stable jobs in citrus farms in Ventura where they had attained seniority, union membership, good wages, and fringe benefits, lost their positions to newer Mexican workers hired at a lower wage and without benefits. Similarly, in a study based on data from the 1980 census, Borjas established a positive correlation between a 10 percent increase in immigration and a 10 percent decline in the wages of immigrants (Borjas 1987).

II

The decline of blue-collar and unskilled jobs began to transform the work force. Reports on schools indicate, for instance, that pure vocational instruction has given way to educational centers that train students to become workers who are capable of competing in a high-tech global economy. Workers formerly trained in manual labor were now being required to have schooling equal to four years of English, writing, math, and science. Trades such as plumbing, mechanics, and masonry no longer depended solely on strength and natural aptitude. Now those fields began to draw more and more on the application of a sophisticated knowledge of technology, mechanical tools, graphic design, and computerized engines. In the world of manufacturing, knowledge of heavy machinery has become less useful than knowing about the abstract notions necessary to grasp the complexity of a changing technology. More importantly, those who once favored changes in vocational schools, asking for curricula that combined skills and strong academics, now decried the federal educational policies of the 1960s. These policies are associated with an ideology that emphasized access and equity without a sufficient concern for performance and the reality of a changing economy.

The increasing requirement in the labor market for skills based on school-related knowledge and language proficiency reduced the likelihood of employment for workers whose educational levels and language abilities were poor. Workers whose abilities did not match the requirements of the labor market were now more likely than before to suffer the decline of blue-collar jobs. They were also less equipped to compete for jobs generated in the new economy. From 1960 to 1990, New York City lost roughly a total of 812,000 jobs in the blue-collar industries. During the same years, the FIRE, services, and government sectors generated approximately 889,000 new jobs, many of which were considered low-skilled positions. The problem with the new low-skilled jobs was not only that there were not enough jobs to meet the demand, but also that even the most menial jobs (i.e., janitor or maid) often required unreasonable qualifications. Many, requiring English proficiency, were simply beyond the reach of those who had poor or no command of the English language. Table 5.1 contains data indicating the level of schooling and English-language proficiency among Dominicans, Puerto Ricans, Colombians, Ecuadorians, and other Latinos during the 1980s. The data show that when compared to pertinent groups, Dominicans have the lowest educational attainment and the least amount of language proficiency, making them less competitive than their Latino counterparts.

The growing demand for services by a highly paid middle class generated a number of unskilled jobs, such as dog-walking, house cleaning, food delivery, and other necessities. This new job market had at its disposal an expanding idle labor force, which included nontraditional workers from every corner of the labor spectrum, holders of various part-time jobs, and college students in need of money for tuition. The intense competition among workers for low-skilled jobs in the service sector is reflected in the fact that menial jobs that once were

TABLE 5.1 **Educational Level and English Language Ability, 1990 (*Persons 16 to 64 years of age*)**

Category	Population Groups				
SCHOOLING	DOMINICAN	PUERTO RICAN	COLOMBIAN	ECUADORIAN	OTHER LATINOS
Mean years of school	9.9	10.8	11.2	10.9	11.2
Less than high school	58.3%	51.6%	39.8%	46.0%	42.5%
High-school diploma	19.3%	24.4%	29.0%	25.8%	24.0%
Some college	16.7%	18.3%	22.1%	21.2%	20.5%
Bachelor's degree	4.0%	3.9%	6.8%	5.4%	7.7%
More than BA	1.8	1.8	2.3	1.6%	5.3%
English Language					
None/poor	45.4%	16.0%	35.6%4	41.1%	27.8%
Very good	20.6%	20.7%	31.6%	24.5%	21.5%
Excellent	34.0%	63.3%	32.8%	34.4%	51.7%

SOURCE: United States Department of Commerce 1994, 1990 Public Use Microdata, Census Sample A.

thought to be reserved for incoming minority immigrants with little formal education, and hardly any proficiency in English, are now held by workers who do not fit that profile.

By 1999 New York still had not regained the level of employment it had in 1989. The creation of jobs in the service industries did not counterbalance the loss of manufacturing and other blue-collar jobs. This trend continued progressively through the 1990s, in spite of the economic recovery that had begun to reflect steady economic growth and record low unemployment levels since the middle of 1996. But it was not only the manufacturing sector; jobs continued to disappear from the FIRE, construction, and the wholesale trade industries, which by the end of 1998 still had less jobs than a decade before. That is to say that an overwhelming expansion of jobs in the service sector has been accompanied by a progressive decline of jobs in other industries. As expected, the sectoral shifting has directly inpacted workers, who have continued to move and be displaced in response to exigencies that emanate from a changing economy. In their analysis of jobs in New York City, Parrot, Meaker, and Nowakowski conclude that "New York experienced a significant degree of structural, as opposed to cyclical, economic change in the 1990s. Several major industries have scaled back employment by 20 percent or more over the last few years, resulting in substantial dislocation. . . . New York's share of dislocated workers is higher in the 1990s than in the 1980s. Whereas worker dislocation declined nationally by 6.7 percent from 1980s to the 1990s, in New York it increased by 21.3 percent" (1999:29).

But the sectoral shifting has also altered the relationship between supply and demand in those areas of the job market that have progressively reduced its need for laborers. In New York displacement has been accompanied by increasing underemployment, or the inability to find jobs in a reasonable amount of time that may permit people to resume control of their lives as productive citizens.[4] Some, perhaps echoing economist Joan Robinson's warnings, fear that the economic changes will inevitably leave some workers out: "High underemployment rates put into question whether New York's labor market can adequately absorb the state's labor force. The underemployment figures suggest that job growth has not been sufficient to keep up with workers' need for employment" (Parrot, Meaker, and Nowakowski 1999:33).

In January 26, 1997, Evelyn Nieves, a reporter with *The New York Times*, wrote that a Salvadoran day-worker had frozen to death on the street in Glen Cove, Long Island. His name was José Santos Fuentes, and some who knew him said he was deeply depressed. At the post where day-workers waited to be selected for a temporary job, Fuentes waited, most times, unsuccessfully. Then he drank and sat alone. A woman told the reporter that "the men would stand in a group by the driveway, but he [Mr. Fuentes] would be over there, thinking, alone." Mr. Fuentes, like many others, was competing against his compatriots for a few bad jobs. Another Salvadoran told the reporter that

"Fuentes came here every day but he hardly found work. It was very difficult." The reporter concluded that "even Mr. Espinal [one of the reporter's informants], who has worked as a day laborer here for 10 years and who speaks English well, has a rough time in the winter. Despite his reputation as a solid worker, the most he can hope to work is three or four days a week. The competition for $60-a-day backbreaking jobs is acute. Yesterday, when Mr. Espinal arrived at the work stop before daybreak, five other laborers were already there. Mr. Espinal looked around an hour later, when two dozen men were milling around, and estimated that 'maybe two or three' would get a day's work" (Nieves 1997:B1).

In October 19, 1999, long before 9 A.M., more than 5,000 people, mostly Hispanics, lined up behind the Bronx County Building in the Bronx. The Bronx is the borough with the largest number of people of Hispanic descent. It is also the county where, since 1990, the second largest concentration of Dominicans live. The people lining up behind the government building were either poorly paid workers or "want-to-be workers" who were simply after a job. The employment histories of the job seekers were diverse, ranging from long-time unemployed workers, presently employed, current welfare-recipient mother to even college graduates. Yet most of them had one thing in common: they were looking for entry-level jobs, either white or blue-collar. Among those who were unemployed, many claimed that they had been looking for months. But their lack of saleable skills turned out to be a problem in finding a job to replace the ones they had lost. Welfare recipients, on their part, knew well that they had to compete for those jobs that did not require the skills they lacked, including speaking English or having a high-school diploma. The forty employers grouped in the largest job fair the Bronx had ever seemed before were looking mostly for workers who had skills: salepersons who spoke English, cashiers who had the ability to handle computerized registers and challenging customers, as well as registered nurses. After a few hours, it became quite clear to many of us that there were too many people after the same kinds of jobs. At the end of the fair, many of those who went there expecting to find a job as movers, delivery persons, messengers, or cleaners, left, hoping to find tomorrow what they were unable to find that day.[5]

Looking for More Than Just Human Capital Qualities

The abundant supply of workers competing for scarce jobs can provide employers with an opportunity to use unscrupulous tactics when hiring a worker to fill certain position. Specifically, it has been suggested that the labor market outcomes of minority workers are affected by discriminatory hiring practices based on the ethnic background of the job seekers in question (Reich 1981; Rodríguez 1991). In the case of unskilled minority workers, their employability is affected by a combination of factors, including the traditional relationship between supply and demand, plus the issue of racial differentiation. The labor market outcomes of skilled and highly educated minority workers, even if they are situated in desirable jobs, could still be affected by their ethnicity.

A 1989 study was conducted in Chicago and San Diego to measure the extent of employment discrimination against persons who "look" or "sound" Hispanic. Pairs of job seekers, one Hispanic and one Anglo, were carefully matched according to credentials, skills, and experience and sent to apply for low-skilled jobs. The outcomes of their search showed a great disparity along ethnic lines: The Anglos received as much as 52 percent more job offers than the Hispanics; three out of every ten employers treated Hispanics unfavorably; and employers granted as much as 33 percent more interviews to the Anglo applicants than the Hispanic ones (Cross et al. 1990:1–2)).

Tables 5.2 and 5.3 contain correlations between earnings, English-language ability, and educational attainment for Dominicans, Puerto Ricans, Colombians, Ecuadorians, and white non-Hispanics. In keeping with the logic of human-capital theory, the correlations show that the more education a worker has and the better she speaks the dominant language, the higher her earnings will be. The evaluation of each individual group considered here provides evidence to substantiate the human-capital notion.

But the paradigm offers only a partial view of the picture. The correlations also show differences in earnings that one cannot explain simply from the standpoint of educational attainment nor ability to speak the dominant language. Overall, the payoff for educational and language achievements is far less for Hispanics than for non-Hispanic whites. Similarly, chances are that if you are Dominican and speak poor or moderate English,

TABLE 5.2 **Mean Earnings+ by English Language Ability, Males, 1989**

POPULATION GROUPS	DOMINICAN	PUERTO RICAN	COLOMBIAN	ECUADORIAN	WHITE NON-HISPANIC
English Proficiency					
Poor	$14,574	$17,958	$17,094	$16,475	$25,150
Moderate	$18,815	$20,548	$19,906	$20,204	$30,385
Strong	$21,420	$23,929	$24,741	$20,448	$44,443

SOURCE: United States Department of Commerce 1994, 1990 Public Use Microdata, Census Sample A.

TABLE 5.3 **Mean Earnings+ by Educational Attainment, Males, 1989**

	Not High-School Graduate	Ratio* %	High-School Graduate	Ratio* %	College Graduate	Ratio* %
Dominican	$15,802	0.61	$20,048	0.44	$21,801	0.40
Puerto Rican	$18,005	0.69	$25,701	0.57	$34,678	0.64
Colombian	$17,142	0.66	$22,202	0.49	$28,975	0.53
Ecuadorian	$17,017	0.65	$20,169	0.45	—	—
White Non-Hispanic	$26,061	1.00	$45,041	1.00	$54,582	1.00

+Mean earnings are calculated for all persons with positive earnings.
*Earnings ratios are calculated by dividing earnings for each group by earnings for non-Hispanic whites.
—Insufficient sample size.
SOURCE: United States Department of Commerce 1994, 1990 Public Use Microdata, Census Sample A.

you would have earnings lower than any worker of another ethnicity who has a similar command of the English language. Similarly, among those with a high-school education or greater,
Dominicans still exhibit lower earnings than each of the groups
compared.

Similar wage disparity among different ethnic groups in New
York City was reported by Parrott, Meaker, and Nowakowski.
These authors found that when comparing non-Hispanic black
males, non-Hispanic white males, Hispanic males, and other
male groups, all of whom had the same level of education, non-
Hispanic whites consistently had the highest earnings in every
one of the four educational categories compared (less than high
school, high school, some college, and college and above). While
Hispanic males had the second highest earnings in three of the
educational categories, and other male groups in two, non-Hispanic black males dominated the second echelon only in one
(some college) (1999:23).

Table 5.4 contains correlations of mean earnings, age, race,
and nativity for Dominicans, Puerto Ricans, Colombians, and
Ecuadorians who were employed full-time in 1990. The figures
show that, other than ethnicity and earnings, the other variables
hold more or less similar values for each one of the groups
compared. They show that among the groups considered,
Dominicans had the lowest earnings, ($14,778). They also had
the lowest and the highest percentages of workers who classified
themselves as whites and blacks (22% and 28%). Clearly, one
cannot draw a cause-effect relationship between race and earnings from the data on the table, but the figures help to discourage a lineal interpretation of the link between human capital
and labor market returns. The study suggests that one should not
ignore the role of racial discrimination against Dominicans in
the labor market. The available data would seem to justify the
hypothesis that if we lined up all the Hispanic subgroups according to skin tone, from the lightest to the darkest, we may find that
excluding Puerto Ricans, whose higher earnings may be influenced by their U.S. citizenship status, the lighter the skin-color of
a newcomer group, the higher the returns to its human capital.[6]

TABLE 5.4 **Selected Demographic Characteristics of Latinos Employed Full Time and Mean Earnings, by Age, Race, and Nativity, in 1990** (*16 to 64 years of age*)

Population Groups	Dominican	Puerto Rican	Colombian	Ecuadorian
Mean Age	36.3	37.3	37.1	35.9
Race (in %)				
White	22.3	43.9	54.1	40.3
Black	28.1	6.1	2.3	2.6
Other	49.6	50.0	43.6	57.1
Nativity (in %)				
Born Abroad	93.8	54.5	94.4	96.8
Mean Earnings	$14,778	$20,159	$17,151	$16,027

SOURCE: United States Department of Commerce 1994, 1990 Public Use Microdata, Census Sample A.

In Sum, the Restructuring of the Economy: No Need for Extra Hands

Post-1965 immigrants to the United States found a troubled economy. But the origins of the problem predated the arrival of the new wave of immigrants. Years ago, some scholars began to note that not every one who wanted to work would find a job. During and after the 1960s, unskilled jobs ceased to be easy to find, while the pool of workers was increasing. The transformation that the labor market was undergoing did not result in a net creation of low- or unskilled jobs that accorded with the growth of the labor force that needed these jobs. The incorporation into the process of production of even a part of the incoming immigrant population had to do primarily with shifts within the contingents of workers, such as labor substitution and discrimination, rather than with an absolute rise in the demand at any given time.

More than thrity years ago, Joan Robinson, a leading British economist, argued that the problem of unemployment in the United States during the 1950s and 1960s had to do with structural causes. Embracing the notion that advanced capitalism

tended to produce an increasing surplus population that the system could not absorb, Robinson warned that "even healthy economic booms [would] leave a considerable 'reserve army'
unemployed" (Robinson 1962:41). Robinson did not see the
problem of full employment as being necessarily connected to
level of investments, as some economists had thought, but rather
to the ability of the means of production to generate enough
jobs. Robinson pointed out the imbalance between supply and
demand as the root of the unemployment problem, contending
that "technical progress [was] continually raising output per
man hour in industry, and the labor force [was] continuously
increasing" (41). She attributed serious consequences to the
inability of an advanced capitalist economy to produce enough
jobs to satisfy the needs of the labor force. As she herself put it:
"The leading capitalist nations [seemed] to be gradually drifting
into the situation of an underdeveloped economy. The characteristic feature of economic underdevelopment is that the system fails to offer jobs to all available workers, not through a temporary *fall* of demand, but for lack of a sufficient increase in the
stock of means of production to employ them. This is the situation in which the United States finds itself now. . . . To preserve
near-enough full employment, market demand must expand as
fast as potential output; merely to prevent it from falling is not
adequate" (42).

The inability of the system to absorb workers who are willing
and able to work represents one of the deepest contradictions
of capitalism. There is simply not a job for every one who wants
one. Capitalist accumulation involves the systematic expansion
of production, as well as the reduction of its cost. While expansion of production leads to mechanization, automation, techni-
fication, the search for new areas of investments, and the transformation of the process of production, the need to reduce cost
brings about the dislocation, substitution, and removal of workers from the process of production. The pool of workers able
and ready to enter the work force constantly increases. The pool
feeds on the addition of new workers, resulting from the bio-
logical reproduction of the population and by the continuous

influx of native workers, who are displaced from other areas of the economy, and from the reservoir of international immigrants, who are, in turn, displaced by the same productive logistic at work in their sending societies.

The economic restructuring of the 1960s emanated from the need to cut the cost of production and widen profit margins. Among the various consequences, the transformation in the production system altered the need for and use of laborers. In the process, the bifurcated labor market with "good jobs" at one end and "bad jobs" at the other, began to be replaced by a new arrangement. Now the labor market increasingly rejected laborers and created fewer jobs to satisfy the employment needs of job seekers.

By the mid-1980s, most companies were contemplating downsizing. By 1990 the United States led all industrialized nations in cutting "good" jobs as a tactic to minimize costs and increase profits. In the 1980s increasing cuts in labor across the board and moderate-to-slow creation of jobs, led to high unemployment rates and an ensuing sense of hopelessness among job seekers. Instead of expecting a secure job market, workers became accustomed to a volatile, evasive, and diffuse market, which has narrowed its capacity to harbor the ever-growing contingent of workers. The changes and effects have been pervasive. The anxiously awaited economic recovery of the last years of the 1990s arrived, at last. But, while some have benefitted from such recovery, many others have not, and they are still waiting for the trickle-down effect some talk about.

The restructuring of the economy and its negative effects on workers and work in the United States have been amply documented. For some scholars, the blame should be laid on a postindustrial capitalist society in which "businesses use new resources to supplement the engineering and production skills identified with the rapid industrialization of the past" (Nelson 1995:4). This society counts on an array of new services and resources, which in the end "reflect the escalating base of capitalism" and the "rising levels of education and expanding literacy of a more professional and specialized white-collar workforce" (Nelson 1995:4). Others believe that the fault lies on a system of production that increasingly neglects people, relies on the use of machinery, and restlessly hunts for profit. Workers are displaced left and right; they are removed from low and top positions, as well. In the process of mechanization, automatization, computarization, and profit hunting, hardly anyone is free from the threat of being sent to the unemployment pool or becoming obsolete. Economist Rifkin argues that "menaced by the increasing intensity of labor's demands and determined to maintain its long-standing control over the means of production, American's industrial giants turned to the new technology of automation as much to rid themselves of rebellious workers as to enhance their productivity and profit" (1995:67). Previously, in a painful analysis of the precarious socioeconomic condition of blacks in the United States, Sidney Willhelm concluded that machines and automatization were competing against blacks, who were being rapidly displaced and were no longer needed in society: "The Negro has always, until present, meant something to the white man. The vast flow of black people entering America came as slaves, a commodity engendering economic investment in black bodies prescribing an economic return; the Civil War transformed the Negro slave into a Negro serf for economic exploitation of labor rather than ownership; now, void of economic returns as either a commodity or a source of labor, the Negro is not only worthless property but also a nonentity from the perspective of White America. For the process of replacing man by machines is now underway, and the Negro is the first *collectivity* to experience the transition" (Willhelm 1971:212–13).

The search for options to reduce cost has entailed an intense and constant mobility of capital. Many new jobs are created in the process, either through science and technology or relocation, but many more are temporarily or permanently destroyed. Jobs are not only mobilized internally, but they are also shipped across the oceans. The internationalization of production and technological improvements stressed the use of cheaper labor in peripheral nations. The mobility of U.S. capital into free-trade zones throughout the Third World, for instance, may not have resolved the unemployment problem in these countries, as many have convincingly argued, but it has lessened the need to import workers here. Companies used to move around to escape negative growth. Subsequently, their movement seemed primarily to pursue higher profits. Yet, in both cases, the move left behind a legacy of job loss and dislocation of workers.

Contesting and Controlling Mass Immigration in the Land of Opportunities

The idea that recent migration to the United States responded to a shortage of labor in given industries whose survival and competitiveness depended on a cheap, insecure, and abundant labor force is challenged by economist Vernon Briggs in *Mass Immigration and the National Interest* (1992). Briggs argues that "beginning in the mid-1960s and accelerating in the decades that have followed, the labor force of the United States entered a period of protracted growth. . . . From 1976 to 1988 the U.S. grew . . . by an astounding 26.5%" (Briggs 1992:203). This growth exceeded by more than one third the labor force growth of nine other leading industrialized nations, including Japan, Germany, France, and the United Kingdom.

Briggs attributed the unprecedented labor force growth to three causes: mass immigration, the rise of females in the labor force, and the maturing of the population. Since immigration has consisted mainly of unskilled and poorly educated job seekers at a time when unskilled blue-collar jobs were declining, and the nation was unable to satisfy the employment needs of unskilled native workers who were increasingly discarded by the process of production, Briggs contends that "there is absolutely no indication that the United States [would] be confronted with the prospect of . . . any shortage of unskilled workers. In fact, no technological advanced nation that has from 20 to 40 million adult workers who are functionally or marginally illiterate need have any fear of a shortage of unskilled workers in its immediate future"(220).

The major reform of the immigration law came in the mid-1960s with the passing of the Immigration Act of 1965 (Hart-Celler Act), which essentially sought to eliminate the national origins system. It has been argued that the new immigration legislation did not intend to increase the number of immigrant workers since "there were widespread fears in Congress at [that] time that increasing the number of immigrants in general would lead to adverse employment and wage effects in the labor market" (Briggs 1992:107). The fears about the negative effects of immigration were stimulated in 1964 by the Republican Party in its campaign discourse during the presidential election. The labor unions lobbying efforts against immigration induced Congress in 1965 to terminate the twenty-two-year-old Mexican Labor Program (the Bracero program).

Immigration reform had been urged for a number of years by members of Congress, as well as by Presidents Truman, Eisenhower, Kennedy, and Johnson. These heads of states had felt that the 1952 Immigration and Nationality Act discriminated against NATO allies of the Eastern and Southern European countries. The 1952 Act essentially encouraged the entrance of people from Northern Europe, particularly from Great Britain, which had received 42 percent of the visas, and from Germany, Ireland, and Scandinavia, which together had received 30 percent. The Southern and Eastern European countries, however, had only received 15 percent of the visas granted to Europeans (Bogen 1987:18–21).

The passing of the 1965 reform had been delayed by a strong and systematic opposition in Congress. Those who had opposed the proposed immigration legislation felt that the 1952 Act allowed the entrance into the country the people best qualified to "preserve the cultural and sociological balance of the country" (Bogen 1987:21). A consensus in Congress was reached in 1965 when the immigration bill was presented to the floor with two important new components: the emphasis on family reunification and the imposition of an annual ceiling of immigration to countries in the Western Hemisphere. The two new components sought to reassure the opposition that immigration reform would not alter the ethnic composition of the country. This was clearly expressed by one of the two congressmen who proposed the 1965 bill, Emmanuel Celler, a Democrat from Brooklyn. Celler, while on the floor urging the passing of the bill argued that "favoring relatives would prevent a rapid shift in the ethnic mix of the new immigrants because their nationalities would match those already here" (Bogen 1987:22). Celler argued that "there will not be comparatively, many Asians or Africans entering the country since the people of Africa and Asia have very few relatives here, comparatively few could immigrate from those countries because they have no family ties to the United States" (Briggs 1992:111).

The 1965 Immigration Act provided equal immigration access to all countries in Europe. Under the new immigration act, the distribution of visas was as follows: 74 percent of the visas were reserved for family reunification, 20 percent for workers with skills needed in the United States, and 6 percent for political refugees. Immigrants admitted under the family reunification provision were subjected to a preference system that contained seven categories. All immigrants not admitted under the family reunification or refugee provisions needed to have a certification from the Department of Labor that their presence was not going to bring any negative effects to the labor market.

The impositions of an annual ceiling of 120,000 for the Western Hemisphere went into effect in 1968. By 1976, concerned over the backlog of applicants seeking visas—especially from Mexico—the 1965 Immigration Act was amended. A ceiling of 20,000 immigrants per any single country and the preference system were imposed on countries of the Western Hemisphere. The modification was intended to control further population movement from this region. Congress feared that, if restrictions were not imposed upon the individual countries of the region, a single country, pressured by internal population increase and economic hardship, could possibly make use of most of the regional quota (Briggs 1992). In addition, the extension of the preference system would limit the likelihood of immigration from the region, since most potential immigrants were related to permanent residents of the United States, who could have only 20 percent of the petitions granted, rather than to U.S. citizens, who had the privilege of petitioning 54 percent of the visa.

Surplus Here, Surplus There, Surplus Everywhere: Displaced Workers and the State

The mobility of Third World workers to the United States after War World II has its root in the workers' home countries. Scholars have shown that workers's emigration has often occurred as a consequence of a direct or indirect involvement of the United States in the economic and political affairs of the sending societies (Portes 1978; History Task Force 1979; Sassen 1988). We argue further that Third World workers constituted, in effect, a surplus labor force in the sending societies, but that their mobility does not necessarily occur in response to a demand for labor in the receiving country. Workers' mobility is viewed differently by those involved in the migration process. One can conclude a priori that for workers, their mobility presupposes a search for economic security; at the same time, the state is released from the responsibility of providing for their well-being or responding to their claims. How immigrants will be judged in the receiving society, however, cannot be viewed with the same degree of certainty. In the absence of a worker's contract, how this migration will be viewed in the receiving society, will depend on whether there is a need for migrant labor and on the kind of citizen rights this society is willing to grant to these workers.

Since 1965 the entrance into the United States of a massive influx of unskilled blue-collar workers from the Third World has received two kinds of responses on the part of the U.S. government. The first can be found in effect from 1965 to 1980, and the second became current beginning in 1980. During the first period, we could say that the entrance of migrants received a sort of "benign neglect." Up to 1980, the year of the Refugee Act, the government seemed neglectful of taking any severe action to restrict or prevent the entrance of unneeded job seekers. Overall, the benign-neglect approach manifested itself in a prevailing permissiveness whereby documented aliens found it relatively easy to settle in poor, working-class communities that received limited social services and other institutional supports. The immigrants did not encounter a sound initiative in place that aimed to enhance their conditions or facilitate their integration. They did not find a labor market with policies designed to synchronize supply with demand to offer them jobs and protect the price of their labor.

During this period, migrant communities were severely underserved in many of their pressing social needs. At the same time, to find work many migrants had to carve out for themselves a space in the informal realm. Others succumbed to employment under irregular and extremely exploitative conditions. In either case, immigrants encountered a receiving society that did very little to ease the obstacles and barriers blocking their normal integration into society. In other words, while the government took no public action to halt the entrance or settlement of immigrants, it remained indifferently passive to their social or labor market needs. This remains true despite the modification of the 1965 Immigration Act in 1976 that aimed to control the immigration of unwanted job seekers strictly through legalistic and procedural means. The benign-neglect approach, with its laissez faire attitude on the part of government authorities had a negative impact on the lives of immigrants.

Up to 1980, then, both the Dominican Republic and the United States opted to deal with the needs of Dominican job seekers in a similar manner. The home country shrugged its shoulders about them and opted to stimulate their emigration, thereby exporting the "problem" while hoping to reap some benefit should the expatriates survive the migratory process. The receiving society, on the other hand, simply decided to deal with "the problem" by allowing the entrance of lawful Dominicans but making no provision to employ them, address their precarious social situation, or to keep them from falling into deep poverty. Both the Dominican and U.S. governments, connected by bilateral agreements related to U.S. investments in the Dominican Republic and exports from the Dominican Republic to the United States, have responded in a similar fashion to displaced Dominican workers: a hands-off policy.

In 1980 we witness a shift in the U.S. government's thinking about Third World immigrants. The benign-neglect approach ceased to be the dominant response to the entrance of unneeded immigrants. Legislative efforts began to be introduced, which proposed a firm attitude toward unwanted job seekers. As the decade progressed, various immigration laws were approved. It became increasingly clear that the State no longer wished to maintain a passive or even merely discursive attitude before the immigrant flows. With the Immigration Reform and Control Act of 1986, which specifically targeted and penalized employers who hired foreign-born workers who did not have proper work authorization, the State initiated a new modality for regulating and controlling the entrance of migrants. Firm, aggressive, and often punitive measures now became part of immigration legislation.

Benign indifference gave way to an aggressive offensive policy against immigrants coming from the Third World, particularly from Latin America and Asia. Legislation was supported by a mass of federal funds. Sophisticated devices such as infrared scopes and eye glasses, helped border patrols to inspect the border with Mexico, which had become an international bridge facilitating the influx of people from Latin America, the Caribbean, and Asia. At the border, tall cement walls were erected to keep intruders out. In addition, the INS employed electrified fences, ferocious and well-trained dogs, special police troops, and other paraphernalia to contain the flow of undocumented immigrants. In the Tucson area, 1,380 agents

were posted in May 2000. Authorities claimed that an overwhelming amount of illegal immigrants were coming in and that
they were catching approximately 900 of them per day. The decision was to secure the area by posting three agents per mile
along the border between the town of Douglas town and the
Naco station, an area which agents believed had been targeted
by incoming immigrants (Zaragoza 2000). In effect, in the town
of Douglas, a citizen who has decided to take action on his own
to help authorities deal with the unwelcome influxes, is offering
tourists a new kind of sporting adventure: a man hunt. The citizen in question is "offering winter vacationers a radical departure from mainstream entertainment. He is inviting winter visitors to come to the Southwest, set their recreational vehicles on
ranch property, and help capture elusive illegal entrants as they
make their nocturnal trek across the Sonoran Desert" (Zaragoza
2000).

While U.S. policies had only targeted undocumented
migrants, in the mid-1990s, the focus expanded to include
documented ones as a pervasive anti-immigration climate
took hold of the land. Spokespersons against documented
immigration raised their voices. Suddenly, policymakers
became concerned about the need for urgent action concerning the nation's surplus unskilled foreign workers. Proposals to curtail immigration flowed forth from government
representatives from the states of Florida, California, Texas,
and Louisiana. In June 1992, Senator Robert C. Byrd shared
this incident with his peers in the Senate: "I pick up the telephone and call the local garage. I can't understand the person
on the other side of the line. I am not sure he can understand
me. They're all over the place, and they can't speak English.
Do we want more of this?" (Sontag 1992:E5). The answer to
his question came in the form of two new laws enacted during
1997: the Anti-Terrorist Act and the Welfare Reform Act. Both
legislative acts have been perceived as anti-immigrant.[7]Since
then, the anti-immigration climate has succeeded in winning
over representative voices from civil society. A national survey
on the issue of immigration conducted by Gallup in 1994

revealed that 65 percent of American people wanted legal immigration curtailed.

The pervasive wave of anti-immigration has reached a peak. Voices adverse to the influx of Third World immigrants are being heard loud and clear in every corner of this country. Washington no longer desires to send an unclear message regarding immigration: unequipped immigrant job-seekers are no longer welcome. Employers have not mounted any opposition. Unwanted job seekers, their children included, must be ready to deal with an inimical atmosphere. Until December 1999, more than 177,000 people had been deported to their countries of origins. Among those deported, some had criminal records indicating minor offences, such as smoking marijuana at a younger age or not paying fare for public transportation. Others who were deported, however, simply lacked proper documentation. The INS has set annual targets for deporting undocumented immigrants and criminals. By 1999, however, INS managed to surpass its own set quota. In 1999 the quota was set at 120,000, which represented a 3 percent increase from the previous year. Yet, in November of the same year, the number of deportees had already reached 57,000 more than the accorded quota for the year (a 142% increase). For now, however, the answer by the sending societies to Washington's immigration policies continues to be formulated according to these countries' needs.

In a presentation at a conference at the CUNY Dominican Studies Institute in New York City, the then Dominican ambassador in Washington, Mr. Bernardo Vega, explained how the new immigration policies had negatively impacted the Dominican Republic. The Ambassador concluded his presentation by urging his compatriots to exercise pressures on Washington to change its immigration policies and to stop deporting criminals back to the Dominican Republic, a society that was unprepared to absorb them and whose laws these people had not violated (Vega 1999). Similarly, the new president of México, Mr. Vicente Fox, in a press conference held at his home in México told reporters that in his upcoming meeting with candidates running for United States President, Governor George W. Bush and Vice President Al Gore, he was going to propose the creation of an open-border policy between México and the United States to facilitate the entrance of Mexican workers, who, in his view, were of vital importance to the U.S. economy.

6.

CONCLUSION: ASSESSING THE PRESENT AND AUGURING THE FUTURE

The United States

The new immigration laws passed by Congress discourage the entrance of unskilled workers into the United States. In a report requested by Congress and released to the general public on December 31, 1997, the General Accounting Office asserted that the country did not face any agricultural shortage of labor. In a telephone conversation with a reporter for *The New York Times*, Dolores Huerta, secretary treasurer for the United Farm Workers, said, "There's definitely a surplus of farm workers. . . . That explains why there has been a drop in farm-worker wages over the past 10 to 15 years. They have dropped wages substantially because they always know there's a large pool of workers they can get" (Greenhouse 1997:A12). In March 25, 2000, the Federal Reserve released a report stating that the median Latino household net worth fell by 24 percent, from $12,170 in 1995 to $9,200 in 1998. Experts estimated that the economic decline was produced by a rapid influx of poor immigrants and a population ill-equipped to benefit from a computer-age economy.

Unions, trade groups, and nativists who opposed immigration have found sympathetic ears in Congress. The bipartisan Commission on Immigration Reform spent five years studying our immigration system. In its final report, released to the public in October 1997, the group celebrated immigrants' contributions to this country: immigrants bring diversity where they settle; they enrich our intellectual and cultural life, and their entrepreneurial abilities create jobs. The same group proposed, however, a reduction of the annual number of legal immigrants admitted and the creation of a new enforcement agency to deal effectively with those who violated laws. Mr. Dan Stein, the executive director of the Federation for American Immigration Reform (FAIR), which opposes any increase in immigration, has energetically raised his voice against what he calls "the flooding of this country with immigrants." FAIR, along with other labor organizations, have called on Congress to reject proposals made by business-interest groups to expand the number of guest-worker programs, which bring in tens of thousands foreigners to work temporarily in the United States.

Immigration policies adopted in the United States since the mid-1980s have begun to have an effect on the number of people arriving from the Dominican Republic. Since 1996 the number of Dominicans admitted to the United States began to decline. In 1998 only 20,387 Dominicans were admitted to the United States. This figure represents less than half the number of Dominicans admitted only seven years before. Unlawful Dominicans residing in the United States have fared no better. The number of those sent back to the Domican Republic has systematically increased in recent years. In 1992, 1,082 Dominicans were deported from the United States. By 1996 this number had increased to 1,916, and by 1998, the latest figure available, the number of deported reached 2,498.[1]

The Dominican Republic

The United States has closed its doors, and people in the Domincan Republic have begun to worry. For many, it is clear that the expatriation of surplus labor offers substantial benefits to the sending country. In the mid-1980s, approximately 60,000 young men and women per year reached legal working age in the Dominican Republic. During the same years, however, the job market could only absorb 7,000 of them. In 1986 historian Frank Moya Pons estimated that the annual exodus to the United States of approximately 25,000 Dominicans greatly mitigated the need to create jobs (Moya Pons 1986:359). If emigration provides a permanent safety valve for the labor market, it also diminishes social tensions and turmoil among unsatisfied Dominicans.

In the eyes of economist Bernardo Vega, a former Dominican Republic ambassador in Washington, unlawful Dominicans should remain in the United States. In August 1999, 8,000 Dominicans were deported from the United States back to the Dominican Republic.[2] The ex-ambassador felt that the expatriation law was unfair. In an interview in the Dominican Republic, Vega commented, "Crimes in the Dominican Republic had increased. The number of criminals was large and this made it difficult to arrest them when they committed crimes [there]" (*El Siglo* 1999:18A).

Dr. Leonel Fernández , who was president of the Dominican Republic at the time, avocated that Dominicans residing in the United States should stay. In a televised message directed to Dominican residents of the United States in the fall of 1997, Fernández urged Dominicans in the United States to become citizens in order to counteract some of the effects of the new immigration law directed specifically at permanent residents. To motivate reluctant Dominicans, President Fernández emphasized that by becoming U.S. citizens, one does not violate one's love for his country or relinquish his patriotic duty (Torres-Saillant 1999:34).

Back in the Dominican Republic, news concerning U.S. Dominicans often deal with Dominicans who return to the island. In general, the presentation is a stereotyped image of U.S. Dominicans. In the imagination of newspapers and magazines, for instance, U.S. Dominicans have been portrayed as

"Dominican-yorks," members of a strange new kind of specimen, who are definitely not Dominicans. The Dominican writer Juan José Ayuso affirms that the Dominican-york who returns "is not the Primitive Dominican who once left, but neither he is the cultured, educated North American" (Ayuso 1994:9). Accordingly, the Dominican-york's dress code, pattern of speech, psyche, and, in general, social behavior, differ dramatically from the national norm in the Dominican Republic.[3]

The new immigration reforms, particularly the Illegal Immigration Reform and Immigrant Responsibility Act of 1996, which, among other things, established a new income requirement for sponsors of legal immigrants, made it more difficult for Dominicans to obtain permanent residence in the United States. The 1996 legislation required a sponsor to have an income that was 125 percent above the poverty line for a family of four. Such a requirement automatically disqualifies the majority of Dominican workers in the United States, whose earnings fall far below the new required income. In 1997 Esteban Delgado reported that, due to the 1996 immigration legislation, 90 percent of the Dominicans who had filed for permanent residence in the United States were likely to be rejected. Delgado, more interested in describing the repercussions of the new law for Dominicans on the island, and not necessarily in providing information concerning the state of poverty in which many Dominicans in the United States live, did not make any explicit comment about the crude reality of most U.S. Dominicans. Yet his article suggested that the overwhelming majority of Dominican people in the United States were simply too poor to sponsor their family members (Delgado 1997:D3). Such a situation, of course, essentially eliminated the possibility of thousands of Dominicans coming to the United States.

In the economic section of a prestigious Dominican newspaper, a headline about population growth in the Dominican Republic reveals that in the Dominicn Republic, many are still tormented by the country's population growth and the surplus labor force. Danilo Rodríguez, the reporter, lamented what he concluded was an "extraordinary rate of population growth" in the Dominican Republic. In his estimation, population growth was the "fundamental cause behind all national problems." Rodríguez concluded that social ills, such as "high unemployment rates, the unequal distribution of wealth, illiteracy . . . the destruction of the forests, the pollution of the rivers, the spontaneous development of marginal neighborhoods located in the periphery of the principal cities, the insufficiency in the provision of energy and drinkable water, the high rates of poverty, the serious health problems, the high incidence of criminality, immorality, the drug-trafficking, the high prices of basic food (including energy), increasing child-prostitution, and the exportation of prostitution" were all caused by population growth in the Dominican Republic (Rodríguez 1997:D2; author's translation). The article ended with a call to the president of the Dominican Republic to help effectively control the population explosion.

The Dominican People

For many Dominicans, however, the need to leave home remains. Poverty and unemployment rates in the Dominican Republic have remained high. In 1993 the Oficina Nacional de Planificación concluded that 60 percent of Dominican homes were poor. Four years later, the same official institution reported that 56 percent of Dominican homes were poor and that almost one in five lived in a state of indigence. As reported in surveys about the concerns of everyday people, most Dominicans seem to be aware of their social conditions. In 1994 a representative national survey conducted by the Pontificia Universidad Católica Madre y Maestra (PUCMM) and the Instituto de Estudios de Población y Desarrollo (IEPD) found that 65.2 percent of the people interviewed (eighteen years of age or older) classified themselves as being poor. A similar survey conducted in 1997 by the same two institutions found that the number of people who classified themselves as poor had increased to 75.8 percent. (Ramírez 1999:2).

In spite of the economic boom during the second half of

the 1990s, unemployment has remained consistently high. In 1993 the unemployment rate in the Dominican Republic was 26.2 percent, and by 1996 it had reached 37.6 percent (Ramírez 1999:8). A study conducted by the International Labor Organization found that the informal economy provided 50 percent of all urban jobs in the Dominican Republic in 1997. The same study found that among all the seven countries studied, the Dominican Republic, with an annual average GNP growth of 4.1 percent, experienced the highest economic growth since 1994 but the lowest growth of the labor force during the same years (Del Cid and Tacsan Chen 1998:12).

As with the survey on poverty, national surveys on popular opinion reveal that most Dominicans are conscious of the lack of jobs in the country. The 1997 survey conducted by the PUCMM and the IEPD found that one third of the people interviewed said that "the major reason behind poverty in the country was the lack of jobs." Corruption among members of the government and the upper class was cited as the second leading cause (25%) (Ramírez 1999:10). In December of the same year, the Gallop-Hoy survey found that 18 percent of those interviewed (18 years of age or older) revealed that "for the forthcoming year, 1998, their wish was to find a job" (Ramírez 1999:10).[4] A year later, in March 1999, the Hamilton-Hoy survey reported that 40 percent of the people interviewed (18 years of age or older) declared that the country's most urgent problem was the need to create more jobs. The agricultural sector was selected by 12 percent of those interviewed as the second most urgent problem affecting the country (Ramírez 1999:10).

Obviously, both the United States and the Dominican governments hold different positions regarding migration. The former writes laws against immigration. The latter, without legislating on the issue, simply acts and undermines what his counterpart does. In the end, if the actions of the Dominican people coincide with the position of either government, it is purely accidental. I suspect that, by now, many Dominicans, whether here in the United States or back in the Dominican Republic, have arrived at a similar conclusion concerning both governments: neither one really cares much for what happens to them or to their children.

All the cards are on the table now. Whether the Dominican power structure will care to make the appropriate adjustments at home to lessen the expulsion of Dominicans is a question worth asking. How much pressure Washington is prepared to exert on the Dominican government to contain emigration is another vital question. One should also ask whether impoverished Dominicans, who have learned to perceive emigration as the route to economic progress, can be expected to simply relinquish that option and risk remaining confined in permanent poverty in their country. The extent to which leaving home may constitute an effective strategy for Dominicans to fulfill their goal of economic progress can only be established after they emigrate, not before. What Dominicans know for sure is that the adventure of emigrating, whatever the perils involved, represents the possibility of hope. For them, the potential to improve their lot is likely to be more appealing than staying home, where the alternatives for socioeconomic progress are slim. My sense is that the adoption of legislation and aggressive measures to stop Dominican job seekers from coming to the United States will not be enough. After all, poor Dominicans have demonstrated that they are not willing to remain in the Dominican Republic while a world of wealth in the form of human resources and financial capital from their country finds its way to the United States. One can safely predict that, if things remain the same back in the Dominican Repubulic and people continue to feel the need to leave, Dominicans will continue to come, whether wanted or not, as long as they think, justifiably or not, that they can change their condition by traveling, legally or illegally, to the United States.

APPENDIX: FIGURES

FIGURE 1. Dominicans Admitted to the United States, 1961–1998

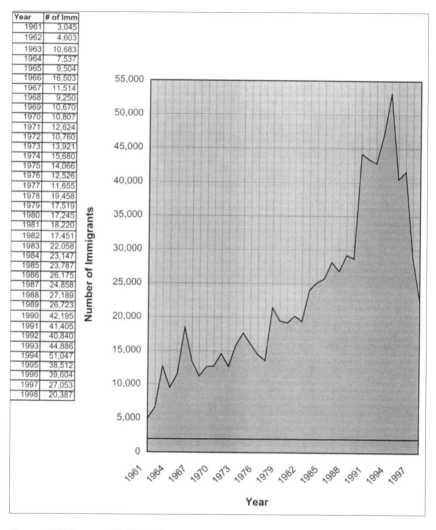

Year	# of Imm
1961	3,045
1962	4,603
1963	10,683
1964	7,537
1965	9,504
1966	16,503
1967	11,514
1968	9,250
1969	10,670
1970	10,807
1971	12,624
1972	10,760
1973	13,921
1974	15,680
1975	14,066
1976	12,526
1977	11,655
1978	19,458
1979	17,519
1980	17,245
1981	18,220
1982	17,451
1983	22,058
1984	23,147
1985	23,787
1986	26,175
1987	24,858
1988	27,189
1989	26,723
1990	42,195
1991	41,405
1992	40,840
1993	44,886
1994	51,047
1995	38,512
1996	39,604
1997	27,053
1998	20,387

Source: INS Reports: 1961–1998.

FIGURE 2. Dominican Republic Fertility Rates, 1950–2000

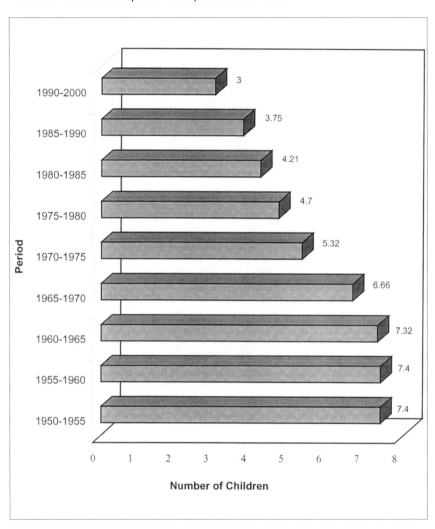

Source: Población y Desarrollo, I (1991):52.

FIGURE 3a. U.S. Consumer Products in the Dominican Market (in US$)

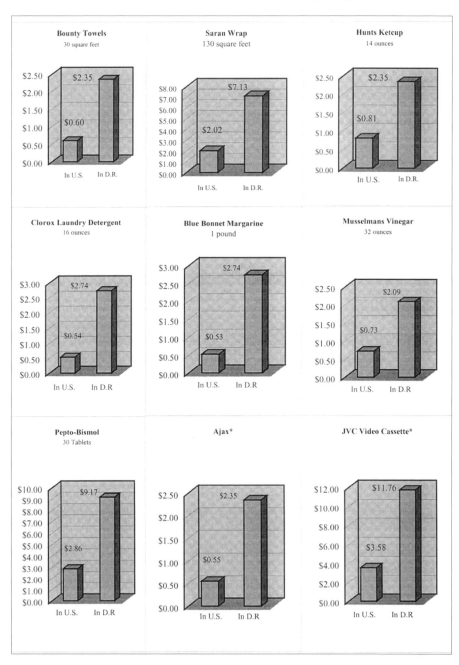

FIGURE 3b. U.S. Consumer Products in the Dominican Market (in US$)

FIGURE 3c. U.S. Consumer Products in the Dominican Market (in US$)

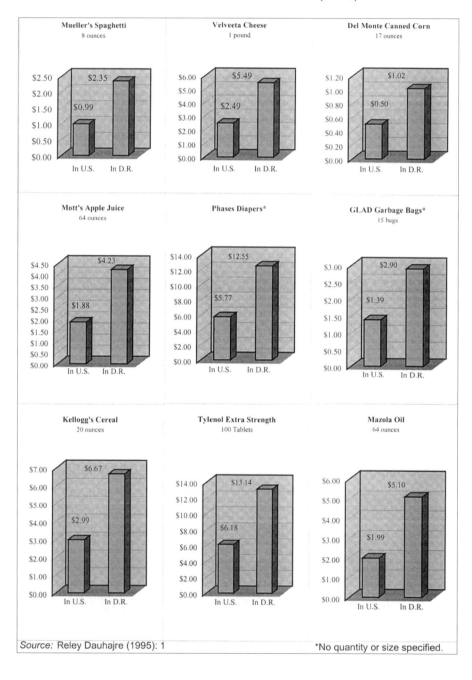

Source: Reley Dauhajre (1995): 1   *No quantity or size specified.

FIGURE 4. Doña Juana's Monthly Income Distribution

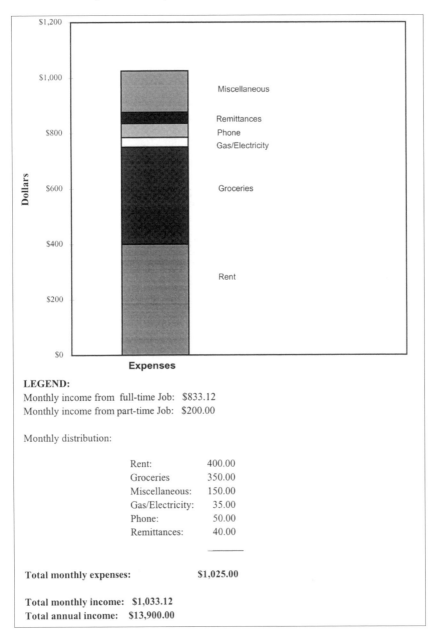

Source: Case study. Interview conducted between October 1996 and March 1997.

FIGURE 5. Unemployment Rates, New York City, 1975–1992

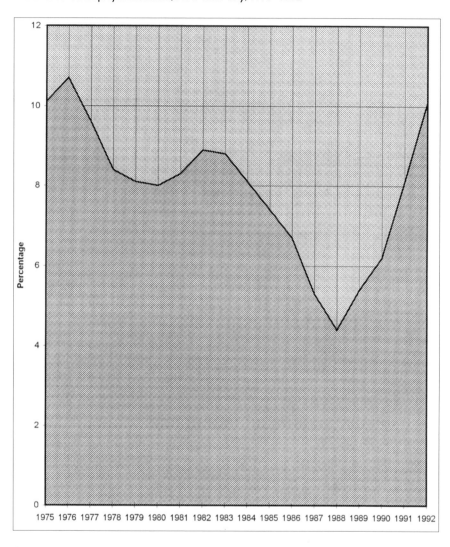

Source: U.S. Department of Labor, Bureau of Labor Statistics, 1975–1992.

FIGURE 6. English Literacy Among Dominicans

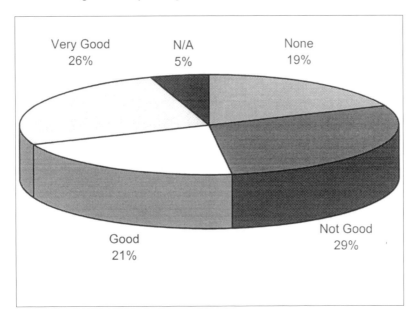

Source: United States Department of Commerce 1994, 1990 Public Use Microdata.

FIGURE 7. New York City Industry Distribution

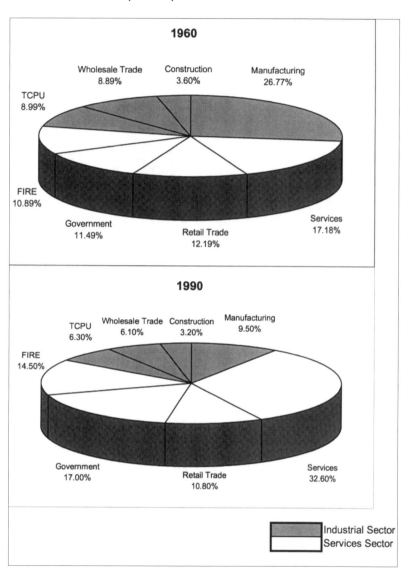

Source: New Opportunity for a Changing Economy (1993): 4.

FIGURE 8. Sectorial Distribution of Employed People, 1960–1991

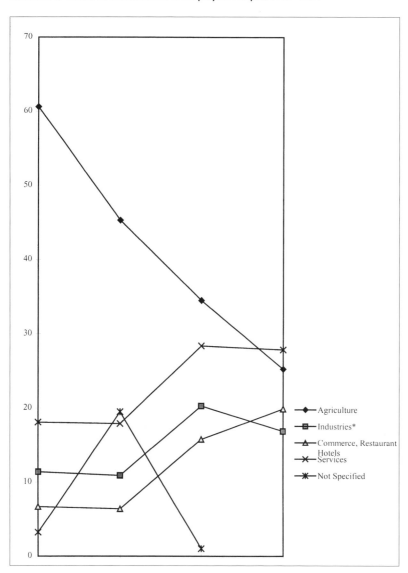

*Includes manufacturing construction, mining, and electricity.
   Source: Ramirez 1993.

Notes

INTRODUCTION

1. In a statistical study concerning Mexico-U.S. migration, Massey and Espinosa disregard the connection between supply and demand in the labor market as an explanation for Mexican migration to the United States. The authors tested forty-one variables and found that there were three leading factors behind Mexican migration to the United States. The first was social capital formation, "which occurs because people who are related to U.S. migrants are themselves more likely to migrate. As a result, each act of migration creates additional social capital capable of instigating and sustaining more migration." The second factor is human capital formation: "The more U.S. experience a migrant accumulates, the higher his likelihood of both documented and undocumented migration." And the third factor is what the authors call "market consolidation": "Growing economic insecurity [in Mexico] coupled with a strong desire to participate in this new political economy [Mexico's economy is intrinsically connected to U.S. and global capitalism] have led Mexican household heads and other family members to migrate internationally as part of a conscious strategy of risk diversification and capital accumulation" (Massey and Espinosa 1997:990–91).

2. Even the view that proposes that migration is produced by a "chain," or in Massey and Espinosa's term, a "social capital formation," one finds a direct connection between jobs and migrants in the receiving society. In chain migration, family and friends who leave home are encouraged by

migrants who possess experiences and relevant information concerning the labor market in the receiving society.

I. THE GREAT EXODUS: ITS ROOTS

1. In 1991 the Dominican Republic was the third leading source country where permanent-resident status was granted to spouses of U.S. citizens and where more than 50 percent of the children of U.S. citizens were born (*Statistical Yearbook of Immigration and Naturalization Service 1991*). Both of these categories are exempted from quota limitations.

2. Sassen's article first appeared in 1979 in *International Migration Review*. I will be using a reprint of the article published in *Caribbean Life in New York City* in 1987.

3. In a study about settlement patterns in fifty U.S. cities, involving eleven new immigrant groups, Richard A. Barff and Dawn E. Hewitt (1989) found that family and friends had a strong influence in determining the locations of Dominicans, Mexicans, and Jamaicans. On the other hand, these authors found that economic variables, such as employment and per capita income, did not have any effect in determining the settlement process of these groups, or that the effect of such variables decreased.

4. Entitled *Statistical Yearbook of the Immigration and Naturalization Service* after 1978. It should be clarified that throughout the years, the number and titles of the occupations listed by INS have been modified a number of times. While eleven occupations were listed in 1970, twelve were listed after 1974, and just eight after 1978. Also, until 1974, proprietors were identified as an occupation and was lumped together with managers and officers. For accuracy, we compared occupations that could be clearly identified as middle, or working, class.

5. For a detailed explanation of the elaboration of law 299, its implications for the different factions of the Dominican bourgeoisie, the role of the United States in its elaboration, and particularly the position of the State, consult Frank Moya Pons, *Empresarios en Conflictos: Política de Industrialización y Sustitución de Importaciones en la República Dominicana* (Santo Domingo: Fondo para el Avance de las Ciencias Sociales, 1992).

6. In January 1997, it was reported on Channel 41, a Spanish television channel in New York City, that a group of women in Texas were protesting against Norplan. The women alleged that the contraceptive had targeted minority women, that it was unsafe, and that it had caused them severe physical damage. According to the news report, the women claimed that most women affected were minority, particularly Hispanic. The reported announced that Norplan had made the product available, free of cost, to minority women, particularly Hispanics, who were unable to pay for it.

2. ECONOMIC GROWTH AND SURPLUS POPULATION

1. Speech cited by Miguel Ceara Hatton in *Tendencias estructurales y coyuntura de la economía dominicana 1968–1983* (Santo Domingo: Centro de Investigaciones Económica, INC.), 57.

2. A *tarea* represents approximately one-sixth of an acre.

3. For 1971 data, consult Carlos Dore y Cabral, *Problemas de la estructura agraria dominicana*, (Santo Domingo: Ediciones Taller, 1982), 19-21. For 1981 data, consult Frank D'Oleo, *1990 Crisis agraria, dominación agroindustrial y descampesinización* (Santo Domingo: Centro Dominicano de Estudios de la Educación, 1991), 31.

4. Conventionally defined as employed full-time people earning less than the established minimum-wage, or who hold jobs that are not commensurable with their qualifications or training, or who, for involuntary reasons, are partially employed without being ill or incapacitated.

5. This terminology for neighborhoods in the city is based on the level of household income. At the time, the established level of household income for a *popular* neighborhood ranged from DR$301 to DR$600, and for a *marginal* neighborhood, it ranged from $50 to DR$300.

6. This calculation is based on the following data. During the 1970s, less than 50 percent of Dominicans reported having an occupation before migrating to the United States. The numbers were 46.8 percent for 1970, 36.5 percent for 1973, 35.7 percent for 1974, 29.3 percent for 1975, 28.0 percent in 1976, and 35.4 percent in 1977. In 1982, out of 17,451 Dominicans admitted, only 6,216 reported having an occupation before migrating to the United States. The number of people who did not report an occupation before migration included housewives and children. For data consult INS reports for the years mentioned.

7. The data for the 1980s was calculated by the author from information provided by the Department of City Planning in *The Newest New Yorkers: An Analysis of Immigration Into New York City During the 1980s* (see source cited). The data included only Dominicans who were sixteen to sity-four years old, and those who did not report an occupation were subdivided into the categories students, unemployed, and homemakers.

3. THE PERCEPTION OF A MIGRATORY MOVEMENT

1. See, for instance, the works of Nancie L. Gonzánlez and Glenn Hendricks cited in this book.

2. It should be noted that when compared with other recent immigrant groups, such as Colombians, Ecuadorians, and Asians, Dominicans tend to exhibit considerably lower labor force participation rates in every age group. Similarly, Pereira et al. (1994) found that in 1990 native-born

Dominicans had the lowest labor force participation rate compared to seven other native-born groups.

3. Acknowledging the long-standing debate among social scientists on the difficulty of agreeing on an operational definition of social poverty, I decided to use the definition provided by the federal government. Some have argued that the poverty line is not an accurate indication of the number of poor people because it does not take into account differences in geographical consumer prices or expenses paid by consumers from their own pockets (such as taxes, child-care costs, medical bills). They propose that a more accurate definition would be based on a family's disposable income, or the amount left after the family has paid taxes and other basic expenses.

4. In this book, the ethnic classifications of Latino and Hispanic are used interchangeably.

5. Since it is likely that every household would have a different number of members, per-capita household income is derived by dividing the total income of Dominican households by the total noninstitutionalized Dominican population.

6. These findings are consistent with the fact that, as explained in chapter 1, those migrating during the 1980s contained a larger number of highly educated migrants (more professional and technical workers) than those migrating during the 1970s. Poverty then is undermined by one's level of skills and formal education rather than by how long one has lived in the United States.

7. James S. Coleman defines social capital "by its function. It is not a single entity but a variety of different entities, with two elements in common: they all consist of some aspect of social structures, and they facilitate certain actions of actors . . . within the structure. Like other forms of capital, social capital is productive, making possible the achievement and certain ends that in its absence would not be possible" (Coleman 1988:98).

8. *Quisqueya*, according to one of the early Spanish chronicles of the European conquest, was one of the names given by the aboriginal population to their land, the island subsequently known as Hispañiola; is currently shared by the Dominican Republic and Haiti. *Platano* (plantain), which belongs to the banana family, along with rice and beans, are the most frequently eaten staples in the Dominican diet.

9. I was taken by Doña Juana to one of these basements. The living arrangements are similar to what is known in the Dominican Republic as *cuarteria*, an informal housing unit in major urban centers, used by the very poor, often uprooted migrants from the countryside, who cannot afford to pay for regular living quarters. The *cuarterias* are normally built in the backyard of a house. The rooms in the basement I visited were of

different sizes and stood one next to the other, separated by plates of chirac. Although each individual unit had electricity, the tenants there paid a common bill charged to the superintendent's apartment, a full unit also located in the basement.

4. DOMINICANS IN THE LABOR MARKET

1. According to New York City's Department of City Planning, between 1990 and 1996, among the top-ten mother's birthplace, the Dominican Republic occupied the number one spot on the list with the highest percentage of births in the city.

2. This study is based primarily on data from census population for 1980 and 1990 and the Current Population Survey for 1996 and 1997. Although the massive migration of Dominicans to the United States began around 1966, it is not until the 1980s that a reliable census sample size could be found. When possible, however, I will make use of data from ethnographic studies that capture Dominicans in the labor market during their early arrival.

3. This chapter will compare Dominicans and aggregate data from major ethnic groups (Hispanics, non-Hispanic whites, and non-Hispanic blacks), and New York City overall. Chapters 3 and 5 look at Dominicans in comparison with Puerto Ricans and other major Hispanic groups in New York City.

4. For a good review of these theories, consult Moss and Tilly's *Why Black Men are Doing Worse in the Labor Market: A Review of Supply-Side and Demand-Side Explanations.*

5. Figures for 1970 are from the 1970 *Statistical Yearbook of the Immigration and Naturalization Service.* Figures for 1982 to 1989 are from *The Newest New Yorkers: A Statistical Portrait,* 1992. 1970 classification of occupations differ slightly from 1980.

6. Immigrants are classified according to the last job held in the sending country or according to the occupation they have been trained for. Source: author's own tabulation from *The Newest New Yorkers: A Statistical Portray,* 69–70.

7. For a detailed analysis of new immigrants in the labor market, consult Pereira et al.: *Labor Force Participation, Occupations and Wages Among New York City Residents: A Comparison of Latinos and Non-Latinos.* Pereira et al.'s report indicates that Dominicans, Colombians, and Ecuadorians tend to occupy the same blue-collar unskilled job markets in the city. Also, *The Newest New Yorkers: An Analysis of Immigration Into New York City During the 1980s* and Waldinger in *Through the Eye of the Needle: Immigrants and Enterprise in New York's Garment Trades* list Chinese workers in the same labor markets.

8. The theoretical explanations for this section are elaborated upon in chapter 5.

5. ON THE INTERNATIONAL MOBILITY OF LABOR

1. A recent approach to the classical equilibrium theory is offered by the household model. Proponents of this model advance the idea that migrants are members of a given household who rationally decide to emigrate to secure economic benefits. In addition, within this model the emigration of people could be conditioned not necessarily by absolute poverty but by relative poverty, or the comparison of members of a given household unit with others in their neighborhood (Stack 1991).

2. For a good review of both theories, see Portes 1978; Wood 1981. In a more recent article, Massey et al. (1994) review both theoretical paradigms and add other variations of these models, such as the household view, the segmented labor-market approach, and the world-system theory. In addition, the authors consider two other views on international migration: the network and cumulative causation. These approaches, however, focus more on the continuation of migration after the movement has begun rather than on the causes that originally led to migration.

3. Studies by Simon, More, and Sullivan 1993; Rivera-Batiz 1991; Grossman 1982; Vroman and Worden 1992 conclud that there was little or no evidence that immigration produced any effect in state-level wages or employment.

4. In the United States, "people are considered underemployed if they are either unsuccessfully seeking work (unemployed), are working part-time but would rather work full-time, are not seeking work because they are discouraged about their job prospects, or have sought work in the past year but are not currently looking for reasons such as child care" (Parrot, Meaker, and Nowakowski 1999:33). Parrot, Meaker, and Nowakowski report underemployment rates in New York in 1998 of 7.1 percent for white males, 12.5 percent for Hispanic males, and 20.3 percent for black males. Hispanic and black females, on their part, had underemployment rates of 19.3 percent and 18.0 percent, respectively, compared to white females, who had an unemployment rate of only 8.3 percent (Parrot, Meaker, and Nowakowski 1999:33).

5. I participated in the job fair pretending to be a Dominican immigrant woman who was looking for a job but who did not know any English.

6. Using 1980 census data, Clara Rodríguez (1991) found that, all things being equal, Puerto Rican males who classified themselves as "other" earned 8 percent less than Puerto Rican males who classified themselves as whites.

7. In July 17, 1996, *The New York Times* reported that many immigrants

who were living legally in the country had been placed in detention by the INS office and faced deportation. Under the new antiterrorism bill, any documented immigrant who has been convicted of a felony, including a misdemeanor like an arrest for smoking marihuana at a young age, is subject to detention and deportation. Similarly, the new Welfare Reform Bill imposed many restrictions on aid to legal immigrants who are not naturalized U.S. citizens. Yet, prowelfare advocates, immigrants, and human-rights groups throughout the country have challenged specific welfare reforms affecting documented children, senior citizens, and disabled immigrants. As a result, some specific measures have been modified to favor documented immigrants.

6. CONCLUSION: ASSESSING THE PRESENT AND AUGURING THE FUTURE

1. These figures represent only those who were actually deported in those years. They do not include those who were eligible to be deported.

2. The number of deportees is provided by *El Siglo*.

3. For a lengthy discussion of the appellative Dominican-york, consult Silvio Torres-Saillant's *El retorno de las yolas: Ensayos sobre diáspora, democracia y dominicanidad* (1999), where he attributes the creation of the term to the Dominican middle class and its need to distinguish themselves from Dominicans in the United States.

4. Expanding the value (18%) to the entire population of similar age in the Dominican Republic, Ramírez, a demographer, estimated the level of unemployment to be around 30 percent in 1998 for that age group in the Dominican Republic.

Works Cited

Abreu, Alfonso et al. 1989. *Las zonas francas industriales: el éxito de una política económica.* Santo Domingo: Editora Corripio.

Amin, Samir, ed. 1974. *Modern Migrations in Western Africa.* Oxford: Oxford University Press.

Ariza Castillo, Marina, et al. 1991. *Población, migraciones internas y desarrollo en la República Dominicana 1950–1981.* Santo Domingo: Impresos Profesionales, C. por A.

Aronowitz, Stanley and William DiFazio. 1994. *Jobless Future: Sci-Tech and the Dogma of Work.* Minneapolis: University of Minnesota Press.

Báez, Clara. 1985. *La subordinación social de la mujer Dominicana en cifras.* Santo Domingo: Editora Montalvo.

Báez Everstz, Franc and Frank D'Oleo Ramírez. 1985. *La emigración de dominicanos a los Estados Unidos.* Santo Domingo: Fundacion Friedrich Ebert.

Blum, David. 1998. "When the Ends Don't Meet; In a City of Fat Cats, Some Wallets Are Paper Thin." *The New York Times,* November 1.

Bogen, Elizabeth. 1987. *Immigration in New York.* New York: Praeger.

Bolton, Reginald Pelham. 1924. *Washington Heights, Manhattan: Its Eventful Past.* New York: Dyckman Institute.

Bonilla, Frank and Ricardo Campos. 1981. "A Wealth of Poor: Puerto Ricans in the New Economic Order." *Daedalus* 110 (Spring):133–76.

———. 1986. *Industry and Idleness.* Hunter College of the City University of New York: Centro de Estudios Puertorriqueños.

Borjas, George J. 1987. "Immigrants, Minorities, and Labor Market Competition." *Industrial and Labor Relations* 40 (3):382–92.

———. 1990. *Friends or Strangers: The Impact of Immigration on the U.S. Economy.* New York: Basic Books.

———. 1992. "National Origin and the Skills of Immigrants in the Postward Period." In George J. Borjas and Richard B. Freeman, eds., *Immigration and the Work Force: Economic Consequences for the United States and Source Areas,* 7–48. Chicago: The University of Chicago Press.

Borjas, George J., Richard B. Freeman, and Lawrence F. Katz. 1992. "On the Labor market Effects of Immigration and Trade." In George J. Borjas and Richard B. Freeman, eds., *Immigration and the Work Force: Economic Consequences for the United States and Source Areas,* 213–44. Chicago: The University of Chicago Press.

Bray, David. 1984. "Economic Development: The Middle Class and International Migration in the Dominican Republic." *International Migration Review* 18(2):217–36.

———. 1987. "The Dominican Exodus: Origins, Problems, and Solutions." In Barry B. Levine, ed., *The Caribbean Exodus,* 152–70. New York: Praeger.

Briggs, Vernon M., Jr. 1992. *Mass Immigration and the National Interest.* New York: M.E. Sharpe, Inc.

Calvo, Felix and Haroldo Dilla. 1986. *Crisis del desarrollismo, auge del monetalismo.* Santo Domingo: Editora Taller.

Candelario, Ginetta E. B, Nancy López, and Ramona Hernández. 1996. "Working Papers on Census Data." Working Group in Migration Studies. CUNY Dominican Studies Institute at City College: City University of New York.

Canelo, Frank J. 1982. *Dónde, por qué, de qué, y cómo viven los dominicanos en el extranjero: un informe sociológico sobre la e/inmigración dominicana, 1961–1962.* Santo Domingo: Alfa y Omega.

Caram de Alvarez, Magaly. 1991. "Cambios en los patrones reproductivos de la familia dominicana." *Población y Desarrollo.* 1:43–60.

Cassá, Roberto. 1982. *Capitalismo y dictadura.* Santo Domingo: Universidad Autónoma de Santo Domingo.

Ceara Hatton, Miguel. 1990a. *Tendencias estructurales y coyuntura de la economía dominicana 1968-1983.* Santo Domingo: Centro de Investigación Económica, Inc. (CIECA).

———. 1990b. *Crecimiento económico y acumulación de capital: consideraciones teóricas y empíricas en la República Dominicana.* Santo Domingo: Universidad Iberoamericana (UNIBE).

Ceara Hatton, Miguel, Elsa Caraballo, Juan José Espinal, Manuel de Jesus Garcia, Apolinar Veloz, José Ramón Brea, and Carlos Rodríguez. 1986. *Hacia una restructuración dirigida de la economía dominicana.* Santo Domingo: Fundación Friedrich Ebert.

Ceara Hatton, Miguel and Edwin C. Hernández. 1993. *El gasto público social de la República Dominicana en la década de los ochentas.* Santo Domingo:

Centro de Investigación Económica y Fondo de las Naciones Unidas para la Infancia.

Cela, Jorge, Isis Duarte and Carmen J. Gómez. 1988. *Población, crecimiento urbano y barrios marginados en Santo Domingo.* Santo Domingo: Fundacion Friedrich Ebert.

Chavez, Linda. 1991. *Out of the Barrio: Toward a New Politics of Hispanic Assimilation.* New York: Basic Books.

Christesen, Kathleen, Alan Foster, and Selin Iltus. 1994. *Contingent Staffing in Small and Medium-Sided Firms in New York City and the Consequences for the City.* New York: The Work Environment Research Group of the Center for Human Environment, Graduate School and University Center of the City University of New York.

Coleman, James S. 1988. "Social Capital in the Creation of Human Capital." *American Journal of Sociology* 94 (Supplement S95):95–120.

Cross, Harry, Geneviene Kenny, Jane Mell, and Wendy Zimmermann. 1990. *Employer Hiring Practices: Differential Treatment of Hispanic and Anglo Seekers.* Washington, D.C.: The Urban Institute.

Del Castillo, José, Miguel Cocco, Walter Cordero, Max Puig, Otto Fernández, and Wilfredo Lozano. 1974. *La Gulf + Western en República Dominicana.* Santo Dominigo: Editora de la Universidad Autónoma de Santo Domingo.

Del Castillo, José and Christopher Mitchell. 1987. *La inmigración dominicana en los Estados Unidos.* Santo Domingo: CENAPEC.

Del Cid, Miguel and Rodolfo Tacsan Chen. 1999. *Fuerza Laboral, Ingresos y Poder Adquisitivo de los Salarios en Centroamérica, Panamá y República Dominicana:1998.* Organización Internacional del Trabajo. Costa Rica: LIL, S.A.

Delgado, Esteban. 1997. "Solicitantes residencia EU deberán tener padrinos." *El Siglo* (November 11):3D.

Díaz, Junot. 1996. *Drown.* New York: Riverhead Books.

D'Oleo Ramírez, Frank. 1991. *1990 Crisis agraria, dominación agroindustrial y descampesinización.* Análisis de Coyuntura. Vol. III, no. 6. Santo Domingo: Centro Dominicano de Estudios de la Educación.

Dore y Cabral, Carlos. 1982. *Problemas de la estructura agraria Dominicana.* Santo Domingo: Ediciones Taller.

Drennan, Matthew. 1991. "The Decline and Rise of the New York Economy." In John Mollonkop and Manuel Castells, eds., *Dual City: Restructuring New York,* 25–41. New York: Russell Sage Foundation.

Duany, Jorge. 1990. "De la periferia a la semi-periferia: La migración dominicana hacia Puerto Rico." In Jorge Duany, ed., *Los dominicanos en Puerto Rico: Migración en la semi-periferia,* 26–46. Puerto Rico: Ediciones Huracán.

Duarte, Isis. 1980. *Capitalismo y superpoblacion en Santo Domingo: Mercado de trabajo rural y ejército de reserva urbano.* Santo Domingo: Colegio Dominicano de Ingenieros, Arquitectos y Agrimensores (CODIA).

Duarte, Isis and André Corten. 1982. "Proceso de proletarización de mujeres: Las trabajadoras de industria de ensamblaje en República Dominicana." Typescript.

Duarte, Isis, André Corten, and Frances Pou. 1986. *Trabajadores urbanos: Ensayos sobre fuerza laboral en República Dominicana.* Santo Domingo: Universidad Autónoma de Santo Domingo.

The Economist. 1990. *Book of Vital World Statistics: A Portrait of Everything Significant in the World Today.* New York: Times Books.

El Siglo. 1999. "Bernardo Vega habla sobre los lazos EEUU-RD." (August 31):18A.

Ellwood, David, Robert Greenstein, and Isaac Shapiro. 1989. "To the Editor." *The New York Times* (April 10):A16.

Emmanuel, Arghiri. 1972. *Unequal Exchange: A Study of the Imperialism of Trade.* New York: Monthly Review Press.

ENDESA (Encuesta Demográfica y de Salud) 1996. 1997. Sai to Domingo: Centro de Estudios Sociales y Demográficos (CESDEM).

Galeano, Eduardo. 1973. *Open Veins of Latin America: Five Centuries of the Pillage of a Continent.* New York: Monthly Review Press.

Garfield, Richard M. and David M. Abramson. 1995. *Washington Heights/Inwood: The Health of a Community.* New York: The Health of the Public Program at Columbia University.

Garrison, Vivian and Carol I. Weiss. 1987. "Dominican Family Networks and United States Immigration Policy: A Case Study." In Constance R. Sutton and Elsa M. Chaney, eds., *Caribbean Life in New York City: Sociocultural Dimensions,* 235–54. New York: Center for Migration Studies.

George, Eugenia. 1990. *The Making of a Transnational Community: Migration, Development, and Cultural Change in the Dominican Republic.* New York: Columbia University Press.

Gilbert, Alan and Josef Gugler. 1982. *Cities, Poverty, and Development: Urbanization in the Third World.* Oxford: Oxford University Press.

Gilbertson, Greta. 1995. "Women's Labor and Enclave Employment: The Case of Dominican and Colombian Women in New York City." *International Migration Review* 29(3):657–70.

Gómez, Carmen J. 1988. "Perfil de las empleadas publicas." *Población y Desarrollo* 23:23–38.

González, Nancie. 1970. "Peasants' Progress: Dominicans in New York." *Caribbean Studies* 10(3):154–71.

——. 1976. "Multiple Migratory Experiences of Dominicans in New York." *Anthropological Quarterly* 49(1):36–43.

González Casanova, Pablo. 1965. "Sociedad Plural y desarrollo: El caso de

México." In Joseph A. Kahl, ed., *La Industrialización en América Latina*, 262–73. México: Editorial F.C.E.

Grasmuck, Sherri. 1985. "The Consequences of Dominican Urban Outmigration for National Development: The Case of Santiago." In Steven Sanderson, ed., *The Americas in the New York International Division of Labor*, 145–76. New York: Holmes and Meier.

Grasmuck, Sherri and Patricia R. Pessar. 1991. *Between Two Islands: Dominican International Migration*. Berkeley: University of California Press.

Greenhouse, Steven. 1997. Report Undercuts Proposal to Import More Farm Labor." *The New York Times* (December 28):A12.

Grossman, Jean Baldwin. 1982. "The Substitutability of Natives and Immigrants in Production." *The Review of Economics and Statistics* 64(4): 596–603.

Gurak, Douglas and Mary Kritz. 1982. "Dominican and Colombian Women in New York City: Household Structure and Employment Patterns." *Migration Today* 10:14–21.

Harris, John R. and M. Todaro. 1970. "Migration, Unemployment, and Development: A Two Sectors Analysis." *American Economic Review* 60:139–49.

Harrison, Bennet and Barry Bluestone. 1988. *The Great U-Turn: Corporate Restructuring and the Polarizing of America*. New York: Basic Books.

Hendricks, Glenn T. 1974. *The Dominican Diaspora: From the Dominican Republic to New York City: Villagers in Transition*. New York: Teachers College Press.

Hernández, Ramona, Francisco Rivera-Batiz, and Roberto Agodini. 1995. *Dominican New Yorkers: A Socio-Economic Profile*. Dominican Research Monograph Series. New York: CUNY Dominican Studies Institute at the City College of New York.

Hernández, Ramona and Francisco Rivera-Batiz. 1997. *Dominican New Yorkers: A Socio-Economic Profile*. Dominican Research Monograph Series. New York: CUNY Dominican Studies Institute at the City College of New York.

Hernández, Ramona and Nancy López. 1997. "Yola and Gender: Dominican Women's Unregulated Migration." In *Dominican Studies: Resources and Research Questions*. Dominican Research Monograph Series. New York: CUNY Dominican Studies Institute at the City College of New York.

History and Migration Task Force, Centro de Estudios Puertorriqueños. 1979. *Labor Migration Under Capitalism: The Puerto Rican Experience*. New York: Monthly Review Press.

Immigration and Naturalization Service (INS). 1960-1991 *Statistical Yearbook of the Immigration and Naturalization Service (Annual Reports)*. Washington, D.C.: Government Printing Office.

Kasarda, John D. 1983. "Caught in the Web of Change." *Society* 21:41–7.

———. 1985. "Urban Change and Minority Opportunities." In P. E. Peterson, ed., *The New Urban Reality*. Washington, D.C.: The Brookings Institute.

———. 1990. "Structural Factors Affecting the Location and Timing of Urban Underclass Growth." *Urban Geography* II:234–64.

Kritz, Mary and Douglas Gurak. 1983. "Kinship Networks and the Settlement Process: Dominican and Colombian Immigrants in New York City." Fordham University. Typescript.

Lantigua, Juleyka. 2000. "Altagracia." Unpublished manuscript.

"Las proyecciones de población en la República Dominicana, 1990–2025." (No date of publication). Santo Domingo: Centro de Estudios Sociales y Demográficos and Oficina Nacional de Planificación Nacional.

López, Nancy. 1994. "Educational Outcomes: The Dynamics of Class, Race, Ethnicity, and Education." *Working Paper*. City University of New York: Center for Urban Research.

Lozano, Wilfredo. 1985. *El reformismo dependiente*. Santo Domingo: Editora Taller.

Magdoff, Harry. 1989. "A New Stage of Capitalism Ahead?." In Arthur MacEwan and William K. Tabb, eds., *Instability and Change in the World Economy*, 349–61. New York City: Monthly Review Press.

Manzueta-Martinez, E. 1994. "Francamente Dominicanas." *Revista Económica del Listín Diario* 3.

Marini, Ruy Mauro. 1973. "Dialéctica de la dependencia: La economía exportadora." In Rodolfo Stavenhagen, Ernesto Laclau, and Ruy Mauro Marini, eds., *Tres ensayos sobre América Latina*, 91–135. Barcelona: Editora Anagrama.

Marshall, Adriana. 1983. "Immigration in a Surplus-Worker Labor Market: The Case of New York." *Occasional Papers* 39. New York University: Center for Latin American and Caribbean Studies.

Marx, Karl and Frederick Engels. 1975. *Ireland and the Irish Question: A Collection of Writings by Karl Marx and Frederick Engels*. New York: International Publisher.

———. 1978. *The German Ideology*. New York: International Publisher.

Martin, John Bartlow. 1966. *Overtaken by Events: The Dominican Crisis from the Fall of Trujillo to the Civil War*. New York: Doubleday and Co.

Massey, Douglas S., Joaquín Arango, and Ali Graeme Hugo. 1994. "An Evaluation of International Migration Theory: The North American Case." *Population and Development Review* 20(4):699–752.

Massey, Douglas S. and Kristin E. Espinosa. 1997. "What's Driving Mexico-U.S. Migration? A Theoretical, Empirical, and Policy Analysis." *American Journal of Sociology* 102(4):939–99.

McCall, Carl H. and Rosemary Scalon. 1995. "Recent Trends in the New York City Economy." New York: State of New York, Office of the Comptroller.

McCarthy, K. and R. Burciaga Valdez. 1985. *Current and Future Effects of Mexican Immigration in California.* Santa Monica: Rand Corporation.

Meillassoux, Claude. 1981. *Maidens, Meal, and Money: Capitalism and the Domestic Community.* Cambridge: Cambridge University Press.

Mill, John Stuart. 1900. *Principles of Political Economy.* London, New York: The Colonial Press.

Mills, C. Wright. 1951. *White Collar: The American Middle Classes.* New York: Oxford University Press.

Mills, C. Wright, Clarence Senior, and Rose Goldsen. 1967. *The Puerto Rican Journey: New York's Newest Migrants.* New York: Harper.

Mines, Richard and Philip L. Martin. 1984. "Immigrant Workers and the California Citrus Industry." *Industrial Relations* 23(1):139–49.

Mitchell, Christopher. 1992. "U.S. Foreign Policy and Dominican Migration to the United States." In Christopher Mitchell, ed., *Western Hemisphere Immigration and United States Foreign Policy,* 89–124. Pennsylvania: The Pennsylvania State University Press.

Moss, Philip and Christ Tilly. 1991. *Why Black Men Are Doing Worse in the Labor Market: A Review of Supply-Side and Demand-Side Explanations.* New York City: Social Science Research Council, Committee on Research on the Urban Underclass.

Moya Pons, Frank. 1977. *Manual de historia dominicana.* Santiago: Universidad Católica Madre y Maestra.

——. 1986. *EL pasado dominicano.* Santo Domingo: Fundación J.A. Caro Alvarez.

——. 1992. *Empresarios en conflicto: política de industrialización y sustitución de importaciones en la República Dominicana.* Santo Domingo: Fondo para el Avance de las Ciencias Sociales.

——. 1995. *The Dominican Republic: A National History.* New York: Hispaniola Books.

Nelson, Joel. I. 1995. *Post-Industrial Capitalism: Exploring Economic Inequality in America.* California: Sage Publications.

Newman, Katherine S. 1995. "What Inner-City Jobs for Welfare Moms?" [op-ed.]. *The New York Times* (May 20).

New York Department of City Planning. 1991. *Annual Report on Social Indicators.* New York City: Department of City Planning.

——. 1991. *Community District Needs: Fiscal Year 1993, Manhattan.* New York City: Department of City Planning.

——. 1992. *The Newest New Yorkers: An Analysis of Immigration into New York City During the 1980s.* New York City: Department of City Planning.

——. 1992. *The Newest New Yorkers: A Statistical Portray.*

New York City: Department of City Planning.

——. 1993. *Socioeconomic Profiles: A Portrait of New York City's Community Districts from the 1980 and 1990 Censuses of Population and Housing.* New York City: Department of City Planning.

——. 1993. *New Opportunity for a Changing Economy.* New York City: Department of City Planning.

Nieves, Evelyn. 1997. A Day Worker, On the Coldest of Nights." *The New York Times* (January 26):B1

Nun, José. 1969. "Superpoblación relativa, ejército industrial de reserva y masa marginal." *Revista Latinoamericana de Sociología* 2:178–235.

Offe, Claus and Rolf G. Heinze. 1992. *Beyond Employment: Time, Work, and the Informal Economy.* Philadelphia: Temple University Press.

O'Neill, Hugh and Mitchell L. Moss. 1991. *Reinventing New York: Competing in the Next Century's Global Economy.* New York City: Urban Research Center, Robert F. Wagner, Graduate School of Public Service, New York University.

Outcault, Sarah. 2000. "Determinant of Fertility Patterns Among Dominicans in the Republic and the United States." Undergraduate thesis, honor's program. University of Massachusetts-Boston.

Parrott, James, Alice Meaker, and Zofia Nowakowski. 1999. *The State of Working New York: The Illusion of Prosperity: New York in the New Economy.* New York: Fiscal Policy Institute.

Pereira, Joseph, Edward S. Cobb, and Amador Roman. 1994. *Labor Force Participation, Occupations, and Wages Among New York City Residents: A Comparison of Latinos and Non-Latinos. Some Findings from Work in Progress.* Herbert H. Lehman College: The Latino Urban Policy Initiative.

Pérez, Glauco. 1981. "The Legal and Illegal Dominicans in New York City." Paper presented at the Conference on Hispanic Migration to New York City: Global Trends and Neighborhood Change. The New York Research Program in Inter-American Affairs at New York University, December 4.

Pessar, Patricia R. 1982. "The Role of Households in International Migration: The Case of U.S.-Bound Migrants from the Dominican Republic." *International Migration Review* 16(2):342–62.

——. 1987. "The Dominicans: Women in the Household and the Garment Industry." In Nancy Foner, ed., *New Immigrants in New York,* 103—29. New York: Columbia University Press.

Pollin, Robert. 1989. "Debt-Dependent Growth and Financial Innovation: Instability in the United States and Latin America." In Arthur MacEwan and William H. Tabb, eds., *Instability and Change in the World Economy,* 121–44. New York City: Monthly Review Press.

Portes, Alejandro. 1978. "Migration and Underdevelopment." *Politics and Society* 8(1):1–48.

Portes, Alejandro and Robert Bach. 1985. *Latin Journey: Cuban and Mexican Immigrants in the United States*. Berkeley: University of California Press.

Portes, Alejandro and Luis E. Guarnizo. 1990. *Tropical Capitalists: U.S.-Bound Immigration and Small Enterprise Development in the Dominican Republic*. Washington, D.C.: Working Papers, Commission for the Study of International Migration and Cooperative Economic Development.

Portes, Alejandro and Luis. E. Guarnizo. 1991. *Capitalistas del trópico: la inmigración en los Estados Unidos y el desarrollo de la pequeña empresa en la República Dominicana*. Santo Domingo: Facultad Latinoamericana de Ciencias Sociales/Proyecto República Dominicana.

Quijano, Anibal. 1977. *Imperialismo y "Marginalidad" en América Latina*. Lima, Perú: Editores Mosca Azul.

Ramírez, Nelson. 1991. *Los cambios en la planificación y la fecundidad en República Dominicana*. Santo Domingo: Instituto de Estudios de Población y Desarrollo.

———. 1993. *La emigración dominicana hacia el exterior*. Santo Domingo: Instituto de Estudios de Población y Desarrollo.

———. 1993. *La fuerza de trabajo en la República Dominicana*. Santo Domingo: Instituto de Estudios de Población y Desarrollo.

———. 1999. "Un país a la medida: distorciones en la medición de la pobreza y el desempleo en la República Dominicana." Santo Domingo: Centro de Estudios Sociales y Demográficos (CESDEM). Typescrip.

Ramírez, Nelson, Antonio Tatis, and Diana Germán. 1982. "Población y mano de obra en la República Dominicana: Perspectivas de la fuerza de trabajo y del empleo-desempleo en el período 1980-1990. *Instituto de Estudios de Población y Desarrollo* 2(1):7–28.

Reinhold, Robert. 1991. "In California, New Talk of Limits on Immigrants." *The New York Times* (December 3):A20.

Rifkin, Jeremy. 1995. *The End of Work: The Decline of the Labor Force and the Dawn of the Post-Market Era*. New York: G. P. Putnam's Sons.

Riley de Dauhajre, Elizabeth. 1995. "Pobre consumidor dominicano." *El Listín Diario, Sábado Económico* (April 29):1.

Rivera-Batiz, Francisco L. 1991. "The Effects of Literacy on the Earnings of Hispanics in the United States." In Edwin Melendez, Clara Rodríguez, and Janis Barra Figueroa, eds., *Hispanics in the Labor Force: Issues and Policies*, 54–75. New York and London: Plenum Press.

Rivera-Batiz, Francisco L. and Selig L. Sechzer. 1991. "Substitution and Complementarity Between Immigrant and Native Labor in the United States." In Francisco L. Rivera-Batiz, Selig L. Sechzer, and Ira N. Gang, eds., *U.S. Immigration Policy Reform in the 1980s: A Preliminary Assessment*, 89–116. New York: Praeger.

Robinson, Joan. 1962. "Latter Day Capitalism." *New Left Review* 16 (July–August):37–46.

Rodríguez, Clara E. 1979. "Economic Factors Affecting Puerto Ricans in New York." In History Task Force, Centro de Estudios Puertorriqueños, ed., *Labor Migration Under Capitalism: The Puerto Rican Experience*, 197–221. New York City: Monthly Review Press.

——. 1991. "The Effect of Race on Puerto Rican Wages." In Edwin Melendez, Clara Rodríguez, and Janis Barry Figueroa, eds., *Hispanics in the Labor Force: Issues and Policies*, 77–98. New York and London: Prenum Press.

Rodríguez, Danilo. 1997. "Una de las causas principales de los males económicos y sociales." *El Siglo* (November 14):2D.

Sanders, Jimy M. and Victor Nee. 1987. "The Limits of Ethnic Solidarity in the Enclave Economy." *American Sociological Review* 52 (December): 745–73.

Santana, Isidoro and Antonio Tatis. 1985. "Tendencias recientes y perspectivas de la situación ocupacional en R.D." *Población y Desarrollo* 9:1–35.

Santana, Isidoro and Magdalena Rathe. 1993. *Reforma social: una agenda para combatir la pobreza.* Santo Domingo: Editora Alfa y Omega.

Sassen, Saskia. 1984. "The New Labor Demand in Global Cities." In Michael Smith, ed., *Cities in Transformation*, 139–71. Beverly Hills, Calif.: Sage.

——. 1987. "Formal and Informal Associations: Dominicans and Colombians in New York." In Constance R. Sutton and Elsa M. Chaney, eds., *Caribbean Life in New York City: Sociocultural Dimensions*, 278–96. New York: Center for Migration Studies.

——. 1988. *The Mobility of Labor and Capital: A Study in International Investment and Labor Flow.* Cambridge: Cambridge University Press.

Serrulle Ramia, José. 1984. *Economia y construcción.* Santo Domingo: Ediciones Gramil.

Simon, Julian, Stephen Moore, and Richard Sullivan. 1993. "The Effect of Immigration on Aggregate Native Unemployment: An Across-City Estimation." *Journal of Labor Research* 14 (Summer):299–316.

Singer, Pablo. 1973. "Urbanización, dependencia, y marginalidad en América Latina." In Manuel Castells, ed., *Imperialismo y Urbanización en América Latina*, 287–312. España: Editorial Gustavo Gili.

Sjaastad, L. 1962. "The Costs and Return of Human Migration." *Journal of Political Economy* 7:80–93.

Sontag, Deborah. 1992. "Calls to Restrict Immigration Come from Many Quarters." *The New York Times* (December 13):E5.

Spengler, J. and G. Meyers. 1977. "Migration and Socio-economic Development: Today and Yesterday." In Alan A. Brown and Egon Neuberger, eds., *Internal Migration: A Comparative Perspective*, 11–35. New York: Academic Press.

Spring William, Bennett Harrison, and Thomas Vietorise. 1972. "Crisis of the Unemployed." *The New York Times Magazine.* (November 5):42–60.

Tactuk, Pablo, Zenón Ceballos, Senaida Jansen, and Maritza Molina Achécar. 1991. "Estudios sobre determinantes, niveles y tendencias de la fecundidad en la República Dominicana." *Población y Desarrollo*1:9–29.

Torres, Andrés. 1995. *Between Melting Pot and Mosaic: African Americans and Puerto Ricans in the New York Political Economy.* Philadelphia: Temple University Press.

Torres, Andrés and Frank Bonilla. 1993. "Decline Within Decline: The New York Perspective." In Rebecca Morales and Frank Bonilla, eds., *Latinos in a Changing U.S. Economy,* 85–108. Newbury Park: Sage Publications.

Torres-Saillant, Silvio. 1999. *El retorno de las yolas: Ensayos sobre diáspora, democracia y dominicanidad.* Santo Domingo: Ediciones Librería La Trinitaria/EditoraManatí.

Ugalde, Antonio, Frank Bean, and Gilbert Cardenas. 1979. "International Return Migration: Findings from a National Survey." *International Migration Review* 13(2):235–54.

United States Department of Commerce. 1983. *1980 U.S. Census of Population and Housing* (Public Use Microdata). Washington, D.C.: Bureau of the Census.

———. 1994. *1990 U.S. Census of Population and Housing* (Public Use Microdata). Washington, D.C.: Bureau of the Census.

———. 1995. *Current Population Survey.* Washington, D.C.: Bureau of the Census.

———. 1997. *Current Population Survey.* Washington, D.C.: Bureau of the Census.

Vega, Bernardo. 1990. *En la década perdida.* Santo Domingo: Fundación Cultural Dominicana.

———. 1999. "Recent U.S. Migration Legislation: Negative Impacts on the Dominican Community." Conference at the CUNY Dominican Studies Institute at City College, April 23, 1999.

Vicens, Lucas. 1982. *Crisis económica 1978–1982.* Santo Domingo: Editora Alfa y Omega.

Vicioso, Chiqui. 1976. "Dominican Migration to the United States." *Migration Today* 20:59–72.

Vroman, Wayne and Kellen Worden. 1992. "Immigration and State Level Wage Adjustments in the 1980s." Washington, D.C.: The Urban Institute. Typescript.

Waldinger, Roger. 1986. *Through the Eye of the Neddle: Immigrants and Enterprises in New York's Garment Trade.* New York: New York University Press.

———. 1996. "The Jobs Immigrants Take" [editorial]. *The New York Times* (March 11).

Weber, Max. 1978. *Economy and Society.* Berkeley: University of California Press.

Willhelm, Sidney M. 1971. *Who Needs the Negro?* New York: Anchor Books.

Wilson, William J. 1987. *The Truly Disadvantaged: The Inner City, the Underclass, and Public Policy.* Chicago: The University of Chicago Press.

Wood, Charles H. 1982. "Equilibrium and Historical-Structural Perspectives on Migration." *International Migration Review* 16(2):298–319.

Zaragoza, Xavier. 2000. "Borane Is Not Amused with 'Ranch Watch' Flyer." *The Daily Dispatch* (April 20):1A

Index

Page numbers followed by "n." or "nn." refer to information in notes.

International Monetary Fund
(IMF), 10, 25, 65–66, 81
IS (Import Substitution): critics of,
56, 73; in Dominican Republic,
52–56, 73–74
IUD, 41. *See also* birth control campaign

job creation: in agrarian sector,
59–60, 81, 82; in Dominican
Republic, 179; in free-trade
zones, 67; intellectual capital in
new industries and, 127; in manufacturing sector, 128–29; in
public sector, 81, 83, 157; in
service economy, 2–3, 124–26,
143, 145, 157–58; State role in,
56; unemployment rates and, 76
job fair, in Bronx, 160–61, 202n. 5
*The Jobless Future: Sci-Tech and the
Dogma of Work* (Aronowitz and
DiFazio), 145
Johnson, Lyndon B., 37, 43

Kasarda, John, 138
Katz, Lawrence F., 155
Kennedy, John F., 46

labor force: contingent workers in,
143–44; DIY displacement of,
146; feminization of, 68; impact
of immigrants on, 155–56;
income and, 69–72, 131–33;
industrial distribution of
Dominican, 127–30; limits of
demand for, 143, 144–48; occupation distribution of, 130–31;
participation rates, 133–36,
199–200n. 2; reasons for growth
of, 168–69; surplus, 35, 60–63,
69–72, 126, 147–48, 164–68, 177;
transformation of skills needed
by, 156–57

labor market: alternative explanations of Dominican outcomes
in, 142–44; bifurcated, supply
and demand, 2–3, 137–38; current explanations of Dominican outcomes in, 138–41;
decline in Dominican Republic,
33; decline in New York City, 6,
122–24, 129, 130, 141, 157; differentiations, explanations of,
136–38; Dominican female participation in, 134–35; Dominican male participation in, 133,
134, 147; "down-graded," 7; English language proficiency and
participation in, 139, 140–41,
157, 158, 162–63, 192; ethnicity
and discrimination in, 161–64;
impact of immigrants on,
155–56; labor mobility alternative theory and, 5–6; residential
patterns and, 141; supply theory of, 137; Washington
Heights, 4–5
*Labor Migration Under Capitalism:
The Puerto Rican Experience,* 40
labor mobility. *See* mobility of labor
labor shortages, 3, 22
Lantigua, Juleyka, 15, 16
latifundios/latifundismo, 35, 56–57
Latinos, income and, 100
Law No. 299 of Industrial and
Incentives Protection, 38–39,
52, 54, 55, 56, 73
literacy, versus education, 137,
140–41. *See also* English language proficiency, labor market
participation and
López, Nancy, 32–33
Lozano, Wilfredo, 38, 64, 78

Magdoff, Harry, 146